The United States and the First World War

We work with leading authors to develop the
strongest educational materials in history,
bringing cutting-edge thinking and best learning
practice to a global market.

Under a range of well-known imprints, including
Longman, we craft high-quality print and electronic
publications which help readers to understand and
apply their content, whether studying or at work.

To find out more about the complete range of our
publishing please visit us on the World Wide Web at:
www.pearsoneduc.com

The United States and the First World War

JENNIFER D. KEENE

Longman

An imprint of **Pearson Education**

Harlow, England · London · New York · Reading, Massachusetts · San Francisco · Toronto · Don Mills, Ontario · Sydney
Tokyo · Singapore · Hong Kong · Seoul · Taipei · Cape Town · Madrid · Mexico City · Amsterdam · Munich · Paris · Milan

Pearson Education Limited
Edinburgh Gate
Harlow
Essex CM20 2JE
England
and Associated Companies throughout the world.

Visit us on the World Wide Web at:
www.pearsoneduc.com

First published 2000

ISBN: 0-582-35620-2 PPR

British Library Cataloguing-in-Publication Data

A catalogue record for this book is
available from the British Library

Library of Congress Cataloging-in-Publication Data
Keen, Jennifer D., 1962-
   The United States and the First World War / Jennifer D. Keene.
     p. cm. -- (Seminar studies in history)
   Includes bibliographical references and index.
   ISBN 0-582-35620-2 (pbk.)
    1. World War, 1914–1918--United States. I. Title. II. Series.
D570 .K38 2000
940.3'73--dc21

                            99-088854

Set by 7 in 10/12 Sabon Roman
Printed in Malaysia, KVP

CONTENTS

AN INTRODUCTION TO THE SERIES

Such is the pace of historical enquiry in the modern world that there is an ever-widening gap between the specialist article or monograph, incorporating the results of current research, and general surveys, which inevitably become out of date. Seminar Studies in History are designed to bridge this gap. The series was founded by Patrick Richardson in 1966 and his aim was to cover major themes in British, European and World history. Between 1980 and 1996 Roger Lockyer continued his work, before handing the editorship over to Clive Emsley and Gordon Martel. Clive Emsley is Professor of History at the Open University, while Gordon Martel is Professor of International History at the University of Northern British Columbia, Canada and Senior Research Fellow at De Montfort University.

All the books are written by experts in their field who are not only familiar with the latest research but have often contributed to it. They are frequently revised, in order to take account of new information and interpretations. They provide a selection of documents to illustrate major themes and provoke discussion, and also a guide to further reading. The aim of *Seminar Studies* is to clarify complex issues without over-simplifying them, and to stimulate readers into deepening their knowledge and understanding of major themes and topics.

NOTE ON REFERENCING SYSTEM

Readers should note that numbers in square brackets [5] refer them to the corresponding entry in the Bibliography at the end of the book (specific page numbers are given in italics). A number in square brackets preceded by *Doc.* [*Doc. 5*] refers readers to the corresponding item in the Documents section which follows the main text. Asterisks mark terms that can be found in the Glossary.

AUTHOR'S ACKNOWLEDGEMENTS

I would like to thank the University of Redlands for providing me with a faculty research grant to write this book, and my husband, Paul Wilkins, for generously reading the manuscript and investing many hours in the tedious work of compiling the bibliography.

PUBLISHER'S ACKNOWLEDGEMENTS

'Beat Back the Hun' poster reproduced courtesy of the National Archives and Records Administration; Plate 4 reproduced courtesy of The Photo Source Ltd., remaining plates reproduced courtesy of the Hulton Getty Picture Collection.

LIST OF ABBREVIATIONS

AEF	American Expeditionary Force
AEFNR	American Expeditionary Force, North Russia
AF of L	American Federation of Labor
BEF	Bonus Expeditionary Force
CND	Council of National Defense
CPI	Committee on Public Information
CTCA	Commission on Training Camp Activities
FTC	Federal Trade Commission
IWW	Industrial Workers of the World
NAWSA	National American Woman Suffrage Association
WIB	War Industries Board
YMCA	Young Men's Christian Association

LIST OF MAPS

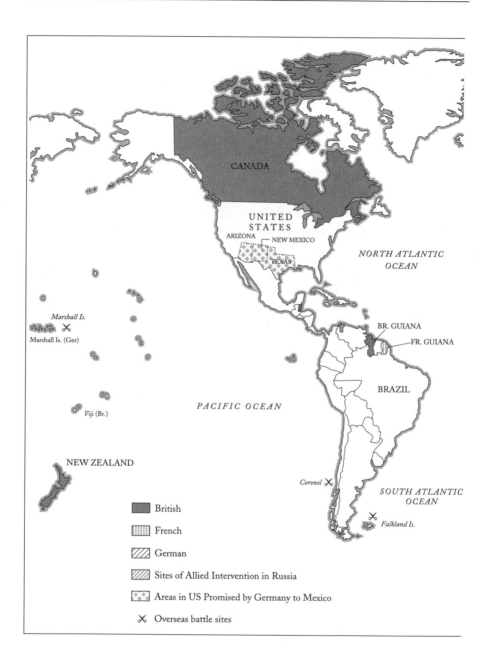

Map 1 World map, 1914–18

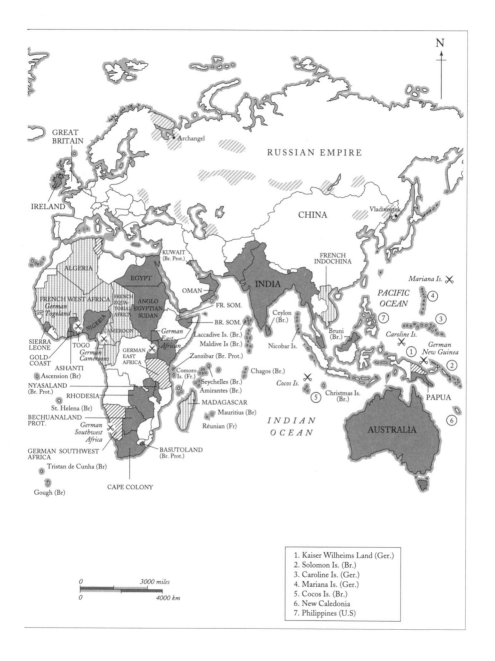

N

GREAT
BRITAIN

• Archangel

RUSSIAN EMPIRE

IRELAND

CHINA

Vladivostok

KUWAIT
(Br. Prot.)

FRENCH
INDOCHINA

Mariana Is. ✗

ALGERIA

EGYPT

OMAN

INDIA

*PACIFIC
OCEAN*

④

FRENCH WEST AFRICA
*German
Togoland*

FRENCH
EQUA-
TORIAL
AFRICA

ANGLO
EGYPTIAN
SUDAN

FR. SOM.

Ceylon
(Br.)

Bruni
(Br.)

⑦

Caroline Is.
✗

③

SIERRA
LEONE

NIGERIA

CAMEROON

BR. SOM.

*German
East
African*

Laccadive Is. (Br.)

Nicobar Is.

*German
New Guinea*

①

②

GOLD
COAST

TOGO
*German
Cameroons*

GERMAN
EAST
AFRICA

Maldive Is. (Br.)

Zanzibar (Br. Prot.)

ASHANTI

📍 Ascension (Br)

Comoro
Is. (Fr.)

Chagos (Br.)

Cocos Is.

NYASALAND
(Br. Prot.)

Seychelles (Br.)

Amirantes (Br.)

⑤

Christmas Is.
(Br.)

PAPUA

RHODESIA

St. Helena (Br)

MADAGASCAR

*INDIAN
OCEAN*

⑥

BECHUANALAND
PROT.

*German
Southwest
Africa*

📍 Mauritius (Br)

Réunian (Fr)

AUSTRALIA

GERMAN SOUTHWEST
AFRICA

BASUTOLAND
(Br. Prot.)

📍 Tristan de Cunha (Br)

📍 Gough (Br)

CAPE COLONY

0 ____ 3000 miles

0 ____ 4000 km

1. Kaiser Wilheims Land (Ger.)
2. Solomon Is. (Br.)
3. Caroline Is. (Ger.)
4. Mariana Is. (Ger.)
5. Cocos Is. (Br.)
6. New Caledonia
7. Philippines (U.S)

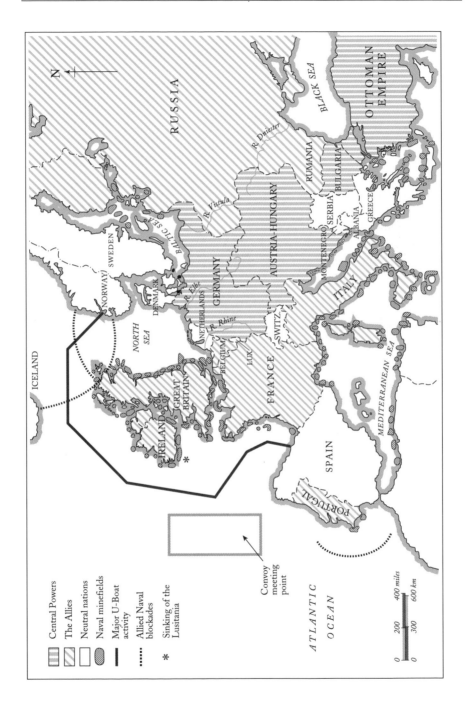

Map 2   Europe, 1914–18

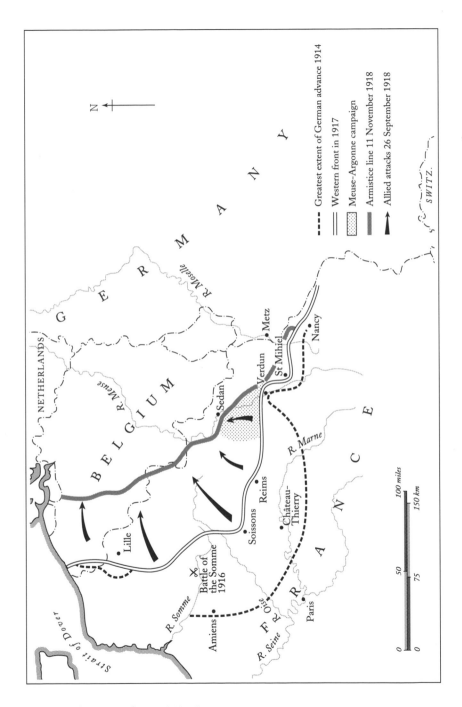

Map 3   The western front, 1914–18

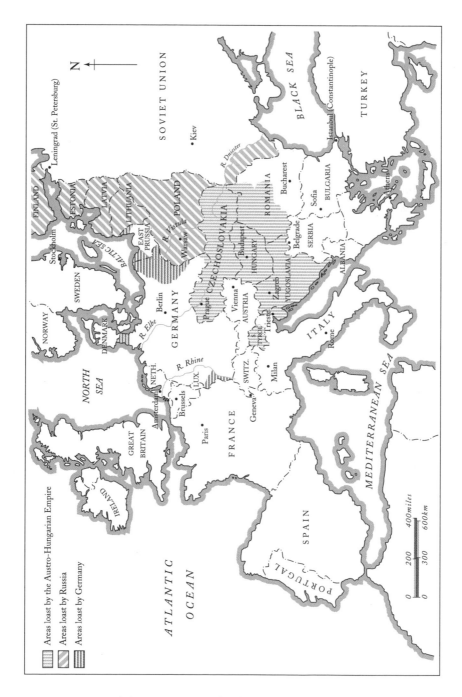

Map 4   Territorial changes in Europe after the First World War

INTRODUCTION

On 28 June 1914 Gavrilo Princip, a Bosnian Serb, came to Sarajevo with five others to assassinate the heir to the Austro-Hungarian throne as he drove through the streets of Sarajevo. Princip belonged to the Black Hand, a Serbian-based Slavic nationalist group that longed for Bosnia to become part of the independent Serbia. He and his fellow revolutionaries believed that Archduke Franz Ferdinand and his wife had deliberately chosen to visit Bosnia on a Serbian national holiday to send the message that Bosnia was, and would remain, an imperial province of the Austro-Hungarian Empire. Their first attempt to assassinate the Archduke was a comedy of errors. The bomb bounced off the side of the car, only injuring two Austrian officers. The police easily arrested the Black Hand member who threw the bomb, and an angry Ferdinand went on to attend the official festivities. Later in the day, the Archduke decided to visit his injured staff members. On the way to the hospital, the driver made a wrong turn down a narrow street and began slowing down to put the car in reverse. Standing at the end of the street was Princip, who could barely believe his good fortune as he saw the slowing automobile carrying the morning's victims towards him. Princip seized the opportunity. He stepped forward and fired, thus fulfilling the morning mission to kill Ferdinand and his wife [55; 63].

The First World War began with these two deaths and ended four years later after nearly fourteen million more. Europeans reacted enthusiastically to the declaration of war. Intoxicating doses of patriotic sentiments and romantic ideals about war prevented most Europeans from taking the time to pause and consider what a general war would mean [122]. Americans, however, followed a completely different road to war. It took two and a half years for the United States to enter the war, and by then there were few remaining illusions about the horror of industrialized warfare. Unlike Europeans in 1914, Americans knew they were deciding for total war when they joined the Allies* in 1917.

The First World War was a pivotal event which had a tremendous effect on the United States, a nation still reeling under the weight and speed of massive changes in its economic, political, and social institutions. Industrial expansion, urbanization, massive immigration, a transportation and communication revolution, the uneasy and imperfect incorporation of free black citizens and immigrants into the national culture, and the nervous acquisition of colonies during the short Spanish-American War of 1898 made the America which went to war in 1917 a very different nation from the one which fought the Civil War. Industrialization made America rich, but the uneven distribution of this wealth became the most encompassing social problem of the time. Labor unrest, urban slums, alcoholism, municipal government corruption, and empire created fertile ground for conservatives, reformers, and radicals to propose different solutions for safeguarding America's future. No one in 1914 bargained on a world war providing many of the answers and direction the country would take.

Debating how to respond to the European war forced Americans to ponder their new status as a world power. The war dramatically illustrated the new threats and opportunities that revolutionized America's relations with the rest of the world in the twentieth century. Throughout the nineteenth century, the Atlantic and Pacific oceans provided a measurable sense of security and detachment from European affairs. This left America free to concentrate on annexing territory in North America with little fear of armed interference from overseas. By the turn of the century, however, the growing importance of international trade to the American economy, the development of faster ships, and the acquisition of a small overseas empire suddenly made the world a smaller place. Americans remembered George Washington's recommendation to avoid entangling alliances, and jealously protected the prerogative to act independently in the western hemisphere established by James Madison in 1823. Still uncertain about what new principles should guide their relations with the rest of the world, Americans hesitated to abandon isolationism and unfettered independence in 1914. The time it took for the United States to decide for war gave President Woodrow Wilson a chance to offer his countrymen a compelling argument in favor of the difference America could make spreading democracy and establishing social justice throughout the world.

Rather than simply presenting an array of factual information, this book examines the war's meaning and significance in American history by evaluating the following questions.

- How did the war change American society? When the war ended, the Constitution had two new amendments, one prohibiting the manufacture of alcohol and the other granting female suffrage. The war's ideological climate posed new challenges to existing amendments to the Constitution, notably the ones guaranteeing civil liberties. For those Americans more interested in supporting than denouncing the war, the wartime economy offered unparalleled opportunities. Reformers, workers, industrialists, and African-Americans all expected the accelerated wartime pace of change to advance their respective causes. Most Americans, however, expected the men who fought the war to return unscathed and to resume their former civilians' lives with little difficulty.

- Did the government use its power appropriately during the war? Before the war, many reformers wanted the federal government to address the social and economic problems plaguing the nation, even if this meant infringing on the rights of property owners. To organize American society to fight a total war, the federal government, among other things, regulated the economy, solved disputes between workers and employers, conscripted an army, suppressed radical dissent, and disseminated propaganda. As a result of these wide-ranging activities, the federal government played an important role in deciding who benefited from the war and who did not. Did these wartime actions fulfill or betray reformers' hopes that the government would use its authority to ensure social justice?

- Would the war give America a permanent role in world affairs? The United States was the only nation whose economy improved, rather than worsened, during the war. Were Americans ready to accept the world responsibilities which went along with this economic power? Having traditionally focused exclusively on the western hemisphere, was America now prepared to accept a fundamental re-orientation in its foreign policy, and become involved in mediating conflicts throughout the world?

These questions relate specifically to the circumstances and legacy of the First World War, but they also fit into the general contours of American history. Throughout its history, the United States has struggled to define an acceptable balance of power between the federal and state governments, sought to reform American society, and retained faith in American exceptionalism. Each time Americans go to war these traditional concerns and aspirations dominate the national conversation. The First World War was no exception to this rule. Finally,

- Was the First World War a just war for the United States?

Evaluating the justness of the war is appropriate because Americans at the time were intensely concerned with this question. President Wilson did his part to present the war as a just one by speaking continuously about the importance of a just peace to justify the unprecedented bloodshed. The nations at war expected the fighting to achieve specific political goals. Each government defended its decision to sanction and organize mass killing as morally sound. Any historical evaluation of the war's origins, strategy, and outcome must also ask if the war was just.

Medieval writers made a useful distinction between *jus ad bellum*, fighting a war for a just reason, and *jus in bello*, fighting a war in a just manner. The two are not necessarily linked. Nations can fight a war for a just cause, but adopt unjust tactics to win. *Jus ad bellum* raises crucial questions about how a society decides for war. Was there a just reason for the United States to declare war on Germany? *Jus in bello* applies to how a society organizes itself for war as well as to events on the battlefield. What are the rules of engagement? Are civilians legitimate targets in time of total war? Does it matter if the war makes some people rich and some people poor? Hopefully, this brief evaluation of the American experience during the First World War will give readers the information they need to decide for themselves if the United States fought a just war in 1917–18.

PART ONE

ORIGINS OF THE WAR

CHAPTER ONE

WAS THE WAR INEVITABLE?

WAR IN EUROPE, 1914

In 1914 Europe was a seething caldron of defensive alliances, distrust, and territorial ambitions [Map 2]. Austria-Hungary and Russia clashed over who would control the Balkans, while Germany challenged the world dominance of France and Britain. Newly arrived on the world scene, Germany was a major industrial power by 1914 and intended to acquire the naval, territorial, and trade possessions which defined a country as a world power. Every French school-boy burned with ambition to avenge the loss of Alsace and Lorraine to the Germans in the Franco-Prussian War of 1870–71. France intended to act quickly to counter any new twentieth-century German threat to their standing as a major world power. In Britain, the government and populace viewed the German ship-building program and the German drive for African colonies with alarm. Map 1 illustrates how this tradition of European imperialism guaranteed that a war based on European disputes would indeed become a world war.

These underlying tensions laid the foundation for the war, but they are not enough to explain why the war occurred when it did. Diplomacy had worked to diffuse other, more direct, recent confrontations between the major European powers. Historians have continuously debated why the Ferdinand assassination led to world war. Was the war due to German expansionist ambitions, the German mistake of supporting Austria-Hungary during the initial crisis, or the collective failure of all European countries to seek a diplomatic solution [63; 128].

After the assassination, the immediate confrontation was between Austria-Hungary and Russia. Austria-Hungary decided to hold Serbia responsible for the actions of a terrorist group which originated from its soil. Russia was determined to continue its support of Slavic nationalism in the region and stand by Serbia in case the Austrian army decided to attack. The German response soon transformed this regional dispute into a global crisis [119; 123]. Germany encouraged Austria-Hungary to send Serbia a set of harsh ultimatums and use the incident to put Serbia in its place. In return,

Germany expected to gain an ally with clear control of the Balkans and access to the Middle East. To many world leaders, including those in Berlin, the crisis appeared over when Serbia accepted all of the Austro-Hungarian demands except one, which demanded that Austro-Hungarian judges come to Serbia to participate in the trials of the terrorists. They were mistaken. Confident of German support, Austria-Hungary had decided to use the assassination as a pretext for annexing Serbia. On 28 July, a month after the assassination, Austria-Hungary declared war on its neighbor. As Austrian naval artillery bombarded Belgrade, Russia resolved to stand by Serbia. The Russian decision to order a general mobilization of its army on 30 July was a fateful one.

Germany viewed Russian mobilization as a direct threat. Map 2 shows why. Ever since the 1894 alliance between Russia and France, Germany had prepared for a two-front war. Alfred von Schlieffen, the German Chief of Staff, had developed a plan which called for Germany to attack and defeat France while the cumbersome Russian army mobilized. Rather than attack France directly along its well-defended borders, the Schlieffen Plan* sent German troops on a northward arch. They were to pass through Belgium first, enter France from the north and then encircle Paris to defeat France within six weeks. Germany could then turn its full forces against Russia without worrying about French attacks to its rear [130]. There indeed was reason to worry about a French attack if Germany went to war with Russia. Once Germany began mobilizing its army, even if it was in response to a threat from Russia, France intended to seek the first-strike advantage by attacking Germany in Alsace.

Now that Russia had begun to mobilize, German military and political leaders decided this was the moment for Germany to break out of the encirclement it had endured for years with enemies on both borders [125; 133]. On 31 July, Germany demanded that Russia cease its preparations for war. On the same day France, Austria-Hungary, and Germany mobilized their armies. After receiving a refusal from Russia on 1 August, Germany declared war on Russia and put a modified version of the Schlieffen Plan into motion. Germany knew it was likely that Britain would feel compelled to stand by its pledge to defend Belgian independence once German troops crossed on to Belgian soil. But Britain's vast global empire and strong navy was of little concern to German officials who envisioned presenting Britain with a *fait accompli*, not initiating a protracted, four-year war of attrition. Therefore, on 3 August, German troops entered Belgium and Germany declared war on France. By 4 August Britain was officially at war with Germany. Austria-Hungary declared war against Russia on 6 August.

Each major European power determined that war was in its national interest in 1914, and all believed they were deciding for a short war of movement [127]. Quickly, however, they realized their miscalculation.

Exhausted by the enormous amount of ground the Schlieffen Plan required them to cover and the difficulties of re-supplying a mass army on the move, the German army ran out of steam along the Marne River thirty-five miles northeast of Paris six weeks after beginning their invasion. A race to the sea ensued, with each side seeking to outflank the other. The result was a defensive line which ran from Switzerland to the North Sea. As each army dug in to defend itself, the war of movement ended and the trench deadlock of the western front began [Map 3]. The European war soon drew in other nations as well. The Ottoman Empire entered on the side of the Central Powers* in November 1914, drawn in by fighting between Britain and Germany in the Black Sea and a Russian invasion [55]. The Italians joined the Allied side in 1915 after receiving guarantees of territorial rewards in the Adriatic. The United States entered on the Allied side in 1917.

Which nation was responsible for starting the war? The question of war guilt would become an important one at the 1919 Paris Peace Conference. In 1914, President Woodrow Wilson believed that all belligerents shared collective responsibility for the war. American views on this question changed, but initially Wilson proclaimed that the United States would remain neutral since there was no just cause or side for Americans to take. Wilson tried to mediate a settlement, but his main interest in 1914 was finding solutions to the domestic problems that concerned Americans much more than any overseas conflict.

WOODROW WILSON: AT HOME AND IN MEXICO

The news of war in Europe shocked the American public, but building a just society at home concerned Americans more than whether or not Europeans were fighting a just war. The idea that a strong government could be used to reform American society was still a new one in 1912 when Wilson took office [165]. Before the Progressive Era (1895–1920), most demands for government action came from the businesses who benefited when the government set high tariffs, distributed western lands to railroads, or sent in troops to break strikes. Progressive reformers, however, wanted the government to defend the economic interests of the common man and the public's welfare. A series of mergers had created huge monopolies in the manufacturing and transportation industries. Progressives wanted government regulation to end unsafe working conditions, child labor, price-setting agreements, and corrupt business practices. To protect their huge profits, industrialists took a new stand against government interference in the economy. They now argued that regulation was a violation of their right to use their private property as they saw fit [159].

Wilson would need the support of both businessmen and reformers during the war, and his pre-war dealings with each group gave them something both to fear and trust in how Wilson used his presidential powers. Wilson's rise to power was a combined tale of unquestioned ability and fortuitous timing. A scholarly man, Wilson was president of Princeton University from 1902 to 1910, then made a successful run for the governorship of New Jersey in 1910. Two years later he was President of the United States. As the Democratic Party candidate, Wilson benefited from the rupture within the Republican Party when former President Theodore Roosevelt decided to run as a third-party Progressive Party candidate against the Republican incumbent William H. Taft. Wilson began his presidency with the intention of using governmental powers sparingly to ensure the continuation of free trade practices. During his first two years in office Wilson lowered the tariff and rationalized the country's chaotic banking practices with the creation of the Federal Reserve system. In 1914, Progressives appeared to score a victory when Wilson supported the creation of the Federal Trade Commission (FTC). Yet the choice of many businessmen as commissioners and the poor record of the FTC in regulating monopolies convinced many reformers that conservative forces had thwarted reform once again [83].

By 1916, for reasons of principle and politics, Wilson embraced many social welfare reforms that a mere four years earlier he had rejected. Pleased with Wilson's new social conscience, Progressives overwhelmingly supported him in his re-election bid. In his second term, Wilson rewarded them by championing a federal child labor law and an eight-hour day for railroad workers. But Wilson could only go as far as the Supreme Court allowed. The power of the Supreme Court to determine the regulatory powers of the federal government became clear when it upheld the eight-hour day for railroad workers in 1917 as within Congress's power to regulate inter-state trade, but struck down the federal child labor law the next year for violating these same principles [165]. During the war, the Court also would determine which expansions of federal governmental power were constitutional and which were not.

The American people concentrated mostly on the role of the government at home, but early on Wilson articulated a clear vision of the American role in the world. 'It would be the irony of fate if my administration had to deal chiefly with foreign affairs,' Wilson noted before his inauguration in 1912, after having focused his campaign on the domestic issues which most interested Americans [139 *p. 19*]. Wilson's pre-war foreign policy decisions revealed that he was dedicated to exporting democracy and to protecting American business interests abroad. He was also willing to use American troops to further both of these goals.

Wilson faced his most critical pre-war crisis in Mexico. The Mexican Revolution began in 1910 when reformer, Francisco I. Madero, overthrew the corrupt regime of Porfirio Diaz. In February 1913 Madero was murdered by one of his generals, Victoriano Huerta. Wilson refused to recognize the Huerta regime and instead offered to aid rebels who pledged to continue Madero's reforms. Venustiano Carranza, leader of the Constitutionalist rebels, refused Wilson's offer because he feared that the Americans wanted to turn Mexico into a client state. Instead, Carranza threatened to fight any American troops which came to depose Huerta. Disregarding Carranza's threat, American troops landed temporarily in Vera Cruz in April 1914 to prevent a German shipment of arms from reaching shore and to exact an apology from the Mexican government for an earlier botched arrest of an American naval crew at Tampico. The intervention precipitated a domestic crisis which forced Huerta to abdicate. Carranza took control of the government, but the country remained divided. Once the Americans recognized the Carranza government, Francisco 'Pancho' Villa, the leader of one rebel faction which refused to support Carranza, was determined to provoke the Americans into sending an army to Mexico. Villa reasoned that if Carranza accepted American military aid he would expose himself as a puppet of the Americans and lose his domestic base of support. If, on the other hand, he resisted American troops then the Americans would finish the job of deposing him [28].

Villa's murderous raids into American border towns soon succeeded in provoking a response from the American army. In 1916, Wilson sent a 12,000-troop punitive expedition under the command of Brigadier General John J. Pershing into Mexico. Their unsuccessful pursuit of Villa eventually drew American troops three hundred miles into Mexico. Wilson mistakenly believed that his Secretary of State, Robert Lansing, had negotiated an agreement with Carranza which authorized the expedition. He had not, and Carranza angrily denounced the American expedition as an invasion of Mexico and demanded the immediate withdrawal of American troops from Mexican soil [165]. Tensions heightened considerably when Carranza ordered his army to stop any further American progress southward. Meanwhile, Wilson mobilized 100,000 National Guardsmen (the reserve troops raised by individual states) to guard the border. A clash between American troops and Mexican government soldiers in Carrizal on 21 June 1916 trapped Wilson between Carranza's demand for immediate withdrawal or war and Congress's call to avenge the deaths of American servicemen by occupying Mexico. Wilson prepared an address requesting permission from Congress to occupy northern Mexico, but then learned that American troops had attacked first at Carrizal. At the brink of disaster, each side blinked. Wilson abandoned his plan to fight Mexico and Carranza released the American prisoners his army had captured. 'Someday,' Wilson told his personal secretary, 'the people of America will know why I hesitated to intervene in Mexico. ... Germany is anxious to have us at war with Mexico, so that our minds and our energies will be taken off the great war across the sea. ... It begins to look as if war with Germany is inevitable. If it should come, I pray God it may not, I do not wish America's energies and forces divided for we will need every ounce of reserve we have to lick Germany' [28 *p. 311*]. The two sides talked throughout the fall, and in January 1917 American troops withdrew [27].

Events in Mexico affected American participation in the First World War in four ways. First, the Mexican crisis illustrated the moral and philosophical underpinnings of Wilson's approach to foreign policy. Secondly, tensions between Mexico and the United States encouraged Germany to believe that an intensified borderland conflict would keep America from entering the European war. American intelligence agents estimated that Germany had spent $12 million trying to provoke a war between the United States and Mexico by encouraging various rebel factions [165]. Thirdly, German espionage in Mexico contributed to Wilson's growing distrust of Germany. Finally, the punitive expedition gave many of the men who would lead the American Expeditionary Force (AEF)* in France their first taste of leading men into combat.

Considering the test to come, the American army appeared woefully unprepared to fight the modern war raging in Europe. In 1916, European armies were facing machine-gun slaughter on an unprecedented scale. Each American infantry regiment, however, only carried four machine guns into Mexico [112]. The limited usefulness of their weekend training sessions became painfully clear when the citizen-soldiers who formed the National Guard arrived to guard the border. To remedy these flaws, the National Defense Act of 1916 increased the size of the regular army and strengthened its role in training the National Guard. The war of movement in Mexico, however, bore little resemblance to the trench stalemate of the western front. The Mexican expedition perhaps did more harm than good by convincing the American army that, having made these small improvements, it was ready to show Britain and France how to fight.

NEUTRAL IN WORD AND DEED, THEN WAR

After two and a half years of neutrality, why did the United States finally decide to fight? The answer to this question in large part determines whether or not the war was a just one. One possible response denies the war a just purpose by claiming that Americans brought the war upon themselves by being anything but neutral from 1914 to 1917. Deciding if the United States was truly neutral requires defining how neutrality is best achieved. Was it the responsibility of the United States to ensure that all sides benefited equally from its resources or simply to hold all belligerent nations to similar standards in how they treated the United States? Those historians more inclined to see the war as a just one insist that German aggression on the high seas challenged American prestige and economic interests and gave Americans no choice but to fight. Another argument which favors the just war interpretation maintains that Americans had a moral responsibility to enter the war since they were the only power capable of establishing a just and lasting peace.

On 18 August 1914, Wilson asked the country to remain neutral in word, thought and deed. From the beginning, however, the United States played a role in the war because both sides bought the arms and supplies that American corporations wanted to sell them. As long as the countries at war had the money to purchase American goods, there was little Wilson could do to hamper this trade except to ban private American bank loans to the belligerent nations. Secretary of State William Jennings Bryan strongly supported this ban because he believed it would 'hasten a conclusion to the war' and keep the United States genuinely neutral [182 *p. 117*]. Wilson, however, lifted the ban in 1915. The warring nations had run short of cash, and the impending cancellation of their orders from American factories and farms threatened to halt the nation's recovery from a recent recession. In theory, all belligerents were eligible for private loans. In reality, American banks loaned funds overwhelmingly to the Allies.

Even if American banks had been inclined to loan more money to Germany, the trade war which was underway between Britain and Germany made it difficult for Americans to trade identically with both sides. The stalemate on the western front caused both Britain and Germany to focus their hopes on disrupting trade to starve the enemy home population and force enemy troops from the field. Britain controlled the seas with its superior navy and used it to establish a blockade* around the Central Powers [Map 2]. Germany depended on the ships of neutrals to transport arms and food bought in the United States [165]. After Britain mined the North Sea, neutral ships could not sail to Germany without first stopping in Britain and allowing a search of their cargo for contraband. The few ships cleared to continue their voyage then received instructions to navigate around the mines [55; 129]. It was an effective blockade since few neutral ships dared enter the North Sea without following the rules established by Britain. By 1916, American trade with Germany was less than 1 percent of what it had been in 1914, but had tripled with Britain and France.

A blockade to prevent war material from reaching an enemy was a recognized, legal weapon of war. The British, however, soon imposed illegal measures such as increasing the contraband list to include food and cotton (not just arms) and blacklisting American firms which traded with the enemy [60; 182]. The neutral nations of Norway and Sweden protested that British tactics disrupted their use of the North Sea and were violations of international law. The American government also officially protested against the blockade on 30 March 1915. In the end, however, the Americans solved their disputes with Britain peacefully. America accepted the illegal blockade of food shipments to Germany with little fanfare. When more vital American economic interests were at stake, such as cotton shipments, Wilson demanded that the British buy enough American cotton to stabilize prices before agreeing to accept its inclusion on the contraband list [165; 182].

The Germans did not have the navy to compete with Britain for control of the seas, but they did have submarines, or U-boats. This new weapon had the potential to reduce severely Britain's access to American goods. The pre-war customs governing trade warfare, however, made the submarine a useless weapon. International law required that the attacking ship stop and search a merchant vessel for contraband, give the crew time to evacuate, and if necessary, take them aboard before sinking the cargo [60]. Yet the key advantage the U-boat offered was its ability to make a surprise attack. Once alerted to the presence of a U-boat, a cargo ship could easily ram and sink it. In addition, by 1915 the British were arming their merchant vessels and these ships did not hesitate to open fire if a U-boat announced its intention to search the vessel. Finally, U-boats were too small for additional passengers [131]. To use the U-boat as an offensive weapon, therefore, meant violating international customs regarding commercial warfare.

On 4 February 1915, Berlin announced a submarine blockade of British waters. The German government warned that since the British had flown the flags of neutrals to protect their merchant ships, all commercial vessels, regardless of the flag flown, risked attack in British waters. Rather than accepting the limitation, and unaware that Germany only had nine submarines with which to enforce this policy, Wilson immediately protested. Wilson denied that it was a double-standard to hold Germany strictly accountable to the rules of international law, but accept illegal British blockade policies [182]. The difference, he claimed, was that British violations did not directly threaten American lives. Because few neutral ships ventured into the mined waters without instructions, the British blockade resulted in minimal loss of life among the nations not officially at war. Bryan argued to Wilson that if Americans and American ships stayed out of the waters patrolled by U-boats around Britain, there was little chance that German U-boats would threaten their lives. The Secretary of State urged Wilson to order Americans to stay off ships headed for the war zone. Ships carrying contraband should not rely upon passengers to protect them from attack, Bryan argued. It was like putting women and children in the front of an army to prevent enemy troops from attacking. But Wilson refused.

On 7 May 1915, disaster struck when a German U-boat sunk the *Lusitania**, a British passenger liner, off the Irish coast. The attack killed 1,198 passengers, including 128 Americans [Map 2]. A series of notes from Wilson demanded that Germany pay reparations and accept the right of Americans to travel on any ship they wished. Wilson ignored requests from

Bryan that he balance his ever-stronger notes to Germany with one pro-
testing British violations of international law or issue a ban on American
travel in the war zone. Bryan consequently resigned on 9 June 1915, rather
than participate in a foreign policy he now perceived as more concerned
with the defense of American neutral rights than with avoiding war [182].
The Germans defended the sinking and pointed out that they had published
warnings to passengers in American newspapers and that the *Lusitania* was
indeed carrying ammunition as part of its cargo. Many German-Americans
agreed [*Doc. 1*]. Eventually, to avoid antagonizing the United States further,
the German government expressed regret over the loss of American lives and
agreed to pay an indemnity.

British propagandists working in the United States ensured that the
American public never forgot the *Lusitania*. Their greatest coup was dis-
covering a coin that they claimed was cast by the German government to
commemorate the sinking. One side of the coin depicted guns and airplanes
going down with the ship and the other side showed Death selling tickets to
passengers under the caption 'Business above all.' Americans believed the
British claim that the bloodthirsty German government issued the coin to
celebrate the deaths of innocent civilians. In reality, a private German citizen
had cast the medal before the ship was sunk. He intended to satirize the
Allied willingness to put civilian lives at risk by using them as shields to
protect their cargo of munitions. Herr Goetz created forty-four medals. British
Naval Intelligence distributed 300,000 copies throughout America [131].

The *Lusitania* sinking was a turning point for the United States. From
this moment on, America's decision about entering the war depended on the
submarine war policy chosen by Germany. In 1915, the Germans decided
against provoking the United States. After another uproar over the sinking
of the *Arabic*, a westbound (hence empty of contraband) passenger ship, on
15 August 1915, the German government renounced its policy of unconditional submarine warfare [124]. On 1 September 1915, in the *Arabic* Pledge,
Germany agreed to refrain from sinking passenger ships with-out warning.

Germany renounced surprise attacks on merchant ships in the *Sussex*
Pledge on 4 May 1916. This pledge came on the heels of another controversial sinking. Eighty passengers perished when a U-boat commander mis-
took a French channel steamer, the *Sussex*, for an armed merchant ship.
Once again, Wilson threatened to break off diplomatic relations. The
German Chancellor, Theobald von Bethmann-Hollweg, convinced Kaiser
Wilhelm II that the submarine was not yet an effective enough weapon to
outweigh the contribution which America could make to the Allied cause
[124]. This restraint concerning surprise attacks on passenger and merchant
vessels paid off. Over the next eight months, German U-boats and raiders
successfully sank over two million tons of Allied shipping without running
the risk of America entering the war [165].

In the *Sussex* Pledge, Germany linked its promise to end surprise attacks on merchant and passenger ships to a demand that the Americans protest British violations of the rights of neutrals. As controversial sinkings ceased, German objections were now heard more sympathetically. The British announcement that it was blacklisting American firms that traded with Germany, British and French inspection of American mail, British back-pedaling on Wilson's peace initiatives, and the brutal suppression of the Irish Easter Rebellion hardened American opinion against Britain in 1916 [165; 182].

True to his conviction that each side bore some blame for the conflict, Wilson tried several times to broker a negotiated peace settlement. Twice, Wilson sent his trusted advisor, Colonel Edward House, to Europe. The first visit in 1915 occurred just as the *Lusitania* went down and, rather than convincing the belligerents to negotiate, this visit convinced House that an Allied victory was desirable. The second visit in 1916 found the British intransigent on the issue of the freedom of the seas, the Germans unmove-able on the issue of submarine warfare, and the French unwilling to consider negotiations until they were closer to victory along the western front. Wilson's final overture for peace came in an address to the US Senate on 22 January 1917 when he called for 'a peace without victory.' In this address, Wilson outlined a plan for a just peace based on 'American principles, American policies,' which he defined as democracy, freedom of the seas, no entangling alliances, and equality of rights among nations. These were, Wilson asserted, '... the principles and policies of forward-looking men and women everywhere, of every modern nation, of every enlightened community. They are the principles of mankind and must prevail' [162 *p. 326*].

By the winter of 1916–17, the effects of the British blockade forced Germany to re-evaluate its policy on unconditional submarine warfare. The Germans called this period turnip winter, a mock tribute to one of the few sources of nourishment available. This time, the German navy won the ear of the Kaiser. The navy argued convincingly that unconditional submarine warfare would cut off the lifeline between Britain and America so quickly that the Allies would capitulate before the American military had time to make any substantial contribution. Consequently, on 31 January 1917, Germany renounced its earlier pledges. Beginning the next day, all ships travelling in the war zone were subject to attack. At first, it seemed that Germany had gambled and won. Wilson broke off diplomatic ties with Germany, but still there was no declaration of war. German submarines began sinking over half a million tons of Allied shipping per month, and the Allies warned Wilson that without these supplies they were doomed. The most Wilson would do, however, was arm American merchant ships so that they could defend themselves from submarine attacks.

The decision to wage unconditional submarine warfare was one of a series of key risks that Germany took to end the war in 1917. The second risk was the Zimmerman telegram* in which German Foreign Minister, Arthur Zimmerman, instructed the German ambassador to Mexico to make a tempting offer to Mexico. The 16 January 1917 telegram claimed that Germany would help Mexico recover Texas, New Mexico, and Arizona (territories lost in the Mexican-American War of 1846–48) if they started a borderland war with the United States and asked Japan to join them. This war would keep the United States busy, protecting its Pacific Island possessions and its southwest border [Map 1]. Coming on the heels of the American withdrawal from Mexico, Carranza was uninterested in this offer. In reality, Mexico could expect little immediate help since it was impossible for Germany to send a military expedition across the Atlantic. The telegram was intercepted by British intelligence agents, and the State Department released the Zimmerman telegram to the press on 1 March 1917. Two days later, charges that this was a British intelligence forgery were silenced when Zimmerman confessed to sending the note [165].

By the time the Zimmerman telegram was published, there was little hope of the United States re-establishing diplomatic relations with Germany. Still, another month passed before Wilson went before Congress to ask for a declaration of war [*Doc. 2*]. On 2 April 1917 Wilson began with a list of Germany's crimes against the international community, noting that 'the present German submarine warfare against commerce is a warfare against mankind' [162 *p. 328*]. He waited until the middle of his address to let the assembled audience hear how he expected the country to react. 'With a profound sense of the solemn and even tragic character of the step I am taking and of the grave responsibilities which it involves, I advise that the Congress declare the recent course of the Imperial Government to be in fact nothing less than war against the government and people of the United States' [162 *p. 329*]. It is important to note that Wilson never requested, nor did he receive, a declaration of war against the Austro-Hungarian or Ottoman empires. The United States did not declare war on Austria-Hungary until 7 December 1917 and did so to prevent Italy from leaving the war after their disastrous defeat at Caporetto. The country was never at war with the Ottoman Empire.

As Wilson was preparing to ask for a declaration of war, Germany was taking its third risk. In April 1917, Vladimir Lenin was part of a group of Russian revolutionaries living in exile in Switzerland whom the Germans sent back to Russia in a sealed train car. Sending dissidents to create internal havoc within an enemy's borders was a strategy pursued by all sides during the war. In the short term, the Russian revolution contributed to the American decision to enter the war. The revolution began in March 1917 when Tsar Nicholas II abdicated his throne. The new provisional government announced its intention to establish a representative government and these political developments removed the last ideological objection that America could not ally itself with an authoritarian government. With democracy now taking root in Russia, Wilson could reasonably portray the war as one in which the democracies of the world were fighting on the Allied side against corrupt Central Power monarchies to determine the future of the world.

In the long run, however, none of the risks taken by Germany in 1917 succeeded as spectacularly as the German attempt to disrupt the course of the Russian revolution. On 7 November 1917, seven months after the United States entered the war, Lenin seized power with promises of peace, land and bread. He immediately fulfilled his first pledge by ending the unpopular war with Germany. Finally, Germany had the opportunity to fight the one-front war it had sought in 1914. Given these ominous developments, by the winter and spring of 1918 it seemed to many in Europe that the Americans had indeed entered the war too late to save the Allied side.

FOURTEEN POINTS AND THE TREATY OF BREST-LITOVSK: JUST VERSUS UNJUST PEACE

In his war address, President Wilson made it clear that he intended the war to be a just one for the country. 'The world must be made safe for democracy,' he proclaimed, and this cause made the war one that the United States must fight [*Doc. 2*]. Was this vision shared by the other nations at war with the Central Powers? Secret Allied treaties, published by the Bolsheviks* after they seized power in Russia, disclosed that this higher goal belonged uniquely to Wilson. In these treaties the Allies had already divided the anticipated conquered territories among themselves. On the heels of this embarrassing revelation, the Bolsheviks invited the Allied nations to state their terms for peace and open negotiations. Responding to this request, Wilson set out to defend the war as a just one whose purpose was to break, not continue, old imperial patterns. On 8 January 1918, Wilson clarified his vision of the just peace settlement that would serve these goals in a speech to Congress which became known as the Fourteen Points* [*Doc. 3*].

The Fourteen Points highlighted differences between how America and the Allies defined victory. The imperialistic and territorial ambitions of Britain and France resonated poorly with Wilson, who was determined to use the war to promote democracy. A year earlier, in his 'peace without victory' speech, Wilson had proclaimed that 'no peace can last, or ought to last, which does not recognize and accept the principle that governments derive all their just powers from the consent of the governed, and that no right anywhere exists to hand peoples about from sovereignty to sovereignty as if they were property' [*162 p. 323*]. In the Fourteen Points, Wilson continued to propose a revolutionary new direction in world affairs with this principle of self-determination. Would his Allies agree that all peoples had the right to a voice in determining their governments or that national boundaries should reflect the ethnic origins of populations? Robert Lansing, who replaced Bryan as Secretary of State, wondered what self-determination would mean for the Irish, Indians, and Egyptians who lived under British rule. What about the conflicting claims between Arabs and Zionists for Palestine? 'The phrase is simply loaded with dynamite,' Lansing noted. 'It will raise hopes which can never be realized' [188 *p. 261*]. Even Wilson was surprised by how many peoples stepped forward to demand the right to determine their own institutions at the Paris Peace Conference in 1919.

Did the Fourteen Points offer the blue-print for a just and lasting peace? Until peace negotiations were underway, few appreciated that the ideal of self-determination fostered nationalism, which in turn undermined the likelihood that nations would agree to other parts of the Fourteen Points, calling for them to give up independent control over trade or the seas [161]. It was not hard for Americans to support freedom of the seas or call on European nations to give up control of the trading routes that made them world powers [136]. Yet Americans were faced with modifying their traditional desire to act unilaterally in the western hemisphere once they joined the League of Nations* that Wilson had outlined in point fourteen.

The Fourteen Points reflected Wilson's belief that existing economic and political arrangements had caused the war. This view was not shared by the French, who blamed Germany for the war, or the British, who blamed the war on the breakdown of diplomacy. The conviction that a new system for handling the world's business was mandatory for a just peace settlement was uniquely Wilson's [153]. Hints of trouble on the horizon were evident when French Prime Minister, Georges Clemenceau, did not even bother to read the Fourteen Points until Germany requested an Armistice* based on them in October 1918. Only the threat of a separate American peace settlement with Germany encouraged France and Britain to accept the Fourteen Points (minus the provision for freedom of the seas) as the basis for the Armistice on 11 November 1918 [184].

The peoples of the world read Wilson's proposals, even if their leaders did not. Wilson's idealism revived hope that a better world might emerge from the bloody débâcle. Even Lenin initially applauded Wilson's vision [139]. Wilson found himself embraced as a man who could single-handedly save the world from its worst impulses. The task ahead was formidable.

Shortly after Wilson issued his Fourteen Points, another model emerged for how the war might end. The Treaty of Brest-Litovsk officially ended the war between Russia and Germany on 3 March 1918. It was the first indication of how unwilling victors might be to fight such a long and bloody war for nothing more than high ideals. This treaty exposed the full imperialist thrust of German war goals when Ukraine, parts of Poland, Finland, Lithuania, Estonia, and Latvia became satellite states of Germany. Russia lost one-third of its pre-war population and arable land, plus most of its coalfields [55]. In addition, Russia was required to demobilize its army and disarm its navy. Reparation payments came in the form of reimbursing Germany for the costs of caring for Russian prisoners of war.

This was a peace of vengeance that reflected Germany's complete victory over Russia. The Brest-Litovsk treaty gave the British and French an idea of the terms Germany might impose on them. This knowledge hardened their resolve to achieve total victory and inflict equally punitive terms of their own [60]. The definition of a just peace, therefore, was still open to interpretation. On the eve of peace negotiations, Clemenceau quipped, 'God gave us his Ten Commandments and we broke them. Wilson gave us his 14 points – well, we shall see' [153 *p. 40*].

CHAPTER TWO

MOBILIZATION: NEW POWERS FOR THE GOVERNMENT

'It wrings my heart when I think of the thousands of American boys that we are going to send to their death', Wilson wrote to the Postmaster General shortly after delivering his war address [188 *p. 230*]. The unpleasant truth, however, was that while some would die, many would profit from this war. Wilson described the nation's international purpose in his war message and the Fourteen Points, but the challenge of directing the country's resources towards winning the war raised critical questions about how the conflict would affect domestic society. How could the government ensure that Americans continued to remain enthusiastic about the war once confronted with the harsh reality of American casualties? How would the country pay for the war? Modern war was expensive and the Americans needed both to fund their own war effort and to continue lending money to the Allies. What was the best way to raise an army? Should the country rely on volunteers, as it had in the Civil War, or use conscription as nations in Europe did? What was the best way to ensure that labor and capital cooperated so strikes or lockouts did not paralyze the war effort? Was it right for business and workers to earn high profits and wages during the war? Would the war set desirable or undesirable precedents for federal government interference in the economy? These were the important questions Americans pondered as they organized their society for war. This chapter will evaluate some of their responses.

BARGAINS AMONG THE STATE, CAPITAL, AND LABOR

America could not mobilize an army, supply, and feed it without granting new powers to the federal government. The development of a government bureaucracy to oversee the wartime mobilization was gradual. In 1916, the first steps towards planning for economic mobilization were taken with the creation of the Council of National Defense (CND). The CND brought together experts from business, financial, and labor circles to advise public officials on mobilizing privately-held industrial resources for national defense [75]. When the nation entered the war, the CND organized over a hundred uncoordinated, cooperative committees charged with hammering out agreements with businesses. The CND, however, had no legal power to enforce these voluntary production codes or regulate the distribution of resources. The growing difficulties that industrialists faced buying raw materials or transporting their goods soon made them more willing to consider centralized governmental direction of the economy [78].

The War Industries Board (WIB) was created in July 1917 and charged with managing the wartime economy. Granting this Washington-based commission the power it needed to direct the civilian economy was a slow process. In the beginning, the WIB was a relatively weak organization without the power to insist that businesses follow its recommendations. By the winter of 1918, the economy was again in crisis. An unusually cold winter created fuel shortages, and grid-locked railroads and ports brought the movement of goods to a standstill [77]. To sort out this mess, Wilson strengthened the WIB in March 1918. The newly-empowered WIB immediately ranked industries to ensure that those most critical to the war effort received raw materials ahead of non-essential wartime businesses. The agency established industrial committees that set prices and standardized production codes. The WIB also became the purchasing agent for Allied governments. Working for the WIB was the first experience in managing the economy for many officials who would go on to serve in the Franklin D. Roosevelt administration during the Depression. In the 1930s, the WIB became the model for the National Recovery Administration, an agency created during the First New Deal* to stimulate economic recovery [79].

The new powers granted to the WIB were significant, but the agency ran into problems when the War Department refused to coordinate their purchases of supplies with the production codes established by the WIB. This stubbornness exacerbated the reigning chaos and confusion. As historian Paul Koistinen notes, 'organizing supply – the civilian economy – was not enough. Demand – the multiple needs of claimant agencies like the army and navy – also had to be controlled' [77 *p. 30*]. The military was a significant purchaser of civilian goods. The army alone consumed $14.5 billion dollars of a total war budget of $32 billion. It took the entire war for the War Department to agree to work with the WIB.

Patriotism abounded during the war, but that did not blind businessmen and labor organizers to the new opportunities now available to them. Government contracts for war goods were quite profitable. Steel, copper, petroleum, meat-packing industries, for instance, enjoyed an increase in profits ranging from 24 percent to 320 percent once they began selling their products to the government [78]. For industrialists, volunteering to serve on WIB industrial committees for a dollar a year offered a chance to establish a friendly relationship with the government [67]. Many businessmen were ready for some permanent restraints on the free-enterprise system, mostly to stop the deadly price-cutting wars which put many smaller enterprises out of business and created an unstable economy which cycled between boom and bust periods. Businessmen, however, wanted a voice in how government regulation was developed, and serving as dollar-a-year men on wartime trade committees gave them influence in setting price, wage, and production codes.

For workers, the war offered the chance to secure high-paying jobs. The government included clauses for high wages in their wartime contracts so the needed material would be produced with as few labor difficulties as possible. In the long run, however, labor's financial gains were not what they seemed at the time. After adjusting for the considerable inflation in consumer goods during the war, real wages only increased four percent [78]. The government also made an historic decision to support the right of workers to organize unions and engage in collective bargaining. This decision temporarily curtailed the government's pre-war tendency to side with factory owners in labor disputes. The placement of labor representatives on wartime trade committees was another indicator of the newly elevated status of organized labor in American society. The hard line the government took against conservative industrialists who refused to recognize unions and its harassment of anti-war radical labor groups helped conservative trade unions like the American Federation of Labor (AF of L) increase their membership by 70 percent between 1917 and 1920 [72]. The federal government, however, made no effort to extend the right to organize unions or collective bargaining to workers in industries unrelated to war production [75].

There were drawbacks for each side, however. Re-tooling a factory for wartime production could mean short-term profits and long-term ruin if businesses completely abandoned civilian customers, distribution networks, and products to manufacture new war-related items for a government market that would end as soon as peace came [82]. The government demanded a no-strike pledge from labor in return for the right to organize and to collective bargaining. Yet the ability to strike was the key source of labor's strength and collective bargaining only worked if the threat of workers leaving their posts induced industrialists to make concessions. Many industrialists paid higher wages because they could pass the cost on to the government. When the war ended and the government canceled its contracts, workers' wartime financial gains disappeared as well.

To manage these competing interests, the government used incentives, threats, direct action, and patriotic appeals to ensure that industrialists and labor served the nation's war needs. Incentives offered to labor included government assurance of fair labor practices and arbitration of labor disputes. The National War Labor Board (made up of representatives from government, business, and labor) required industries that accepted government contracts to honor the eight-hour day and forty-hour week, pay a living wage, maintain high safety standards in factories, recognize the union's right to recruit members at work, and eliminate blacklists which barred union members from employment [66]. By sticking to these principles in numerous arbitration cases, the Board won the wartime reputation for promoting social justice, not just full production. If these incentives were not enough to attract young male workers to war-related jobs, there were possible punitive consequences. The 'work or fight' clause in the 1918 Selective Service Act gave the government the power to revoke the draft exemptions of able-bodied single male workers if they quit their industrial jobs [98].

Business received its own version of the government's carrot-and-stick approach. The War Finance Corporation, for example, extended loans or credit to businesses who agreed to supply the war effort [82]. As WIB Chairman, Bernard Baruch, noted, however, the power to channel supplies to cooperative industrialists was 'the iron fist in the velvet glove' [67 *p. 191*]. Steel deliveries, for example, went primarily to automakers who produced military vehicles. A car manufacturer either switched to wartime production or went out of business. The combined incentive of loans to help automakers re-tool their factories, ample profits in wartime contracts, and the threat of losing access to raw materials reduced the production of leisure cars by 75 percent during the war.

Direct action was the most dramatic, and least used, alternative. The government's most daring use of its wartime powers was the decision on 26 December 1917 to take over the railroads. The government now controlled the equipment and staff of a few hundred railroad companies and 240,000 miles of track. By the time the government intervened, rail traffic was at a standstill in the east. The union brotherhoods were preparing to strike, skilled railway workers were leaving in droves for better industrial jobs, and fuel shortages hampered train movement. Ensuring the smooth functioning of the railroads was the first priority of the new Railroad Administration, led by Secretary of the Treasury William G. McAdoo. McAdoo, however, was also determined to modernize and rationalize the nation's railway system. The government standardized equipment, coordinated the use of tracks, and, where possible, placed competing passenger lines under the roof of one city terminal. Yet, even this coercive act was smoothed over with money [75]. The government amply rewarded railroad companies by renting their equipment for a generous sum and compensating them for wear and tear. At the end of the war, labor unions pressed for the permanent nationalization of the railroads but the government returned the railroads to their owners in 1920. When the new Railway Labor Board (created by the

Transportation Act of 1920) voted to reduce wages and supported an injunction against a strike, railroad workers knew that the pre-war pattern of the government siding with business in labor disputes had returned.

On the other end of the spectrum lay the policies pursued by the Food Administration. Congress gave the President near dictatorial powers to regulate the food and fuel industries in the 1917 Lever Food and Fuel Act. Food Administrator Herbert Hoover, however, rejected rationing or price controls. He instead relied on high prices and patriotism to control the nation's food supply. To stimulate production, Hoover forced the American and Allied governments to pay high prices for agricultural goods. To curb civilian demand, Hoover organized a propaganda campaign around the slogan 'food will win the war' to encourage wheatless Mondays, meatless Tuesdays, and porkless Saturdays. Hoover's approach was based on incentives and voluntarism. There was no question that to most Americans these indirect tactics were more acceptable than the direct government takeover of the railroads. Hoover's actions, however, set in motion events that would come back to haunt him during his presidency. Many farmers went into debt during the war to expand production and take advantage of high prices for agricultural goods [184]. Though farmers increased their profit margin by 25 percent during the war, their failure to anticipate a post-war recession hurt them dramatically [162]. For American farmers the depression began in 1919, not ten years later when the stock market crashed. As President, Hoover would find himself reversing his wartime position and urging farmers to constrict their production to raise agricultural prices.

Harry Garfield, the head of the Fuel Administration, relied on a mix of enticements, coercion and voluntarism. Garfield asked Americans to observe heatless Thursdays and set high prices and subsidies for coal to stimulate production. He did not hesitate, however, to close all non-war-related industries which used bituminous coal in January 1918 until the government's takeover of the railroads untangled the gridlock creating fuel shortages [80]. The Fuel Administration also used its right to set priorities in shipments to direct oil from civilian to military uses.

Was the mobilization of the economy efficient? All these agencies performed well if the measure was ensuring the timely mobilization of the nation's manufacturing, transportation, food, and fuel resources for military purposes. Another criterion upon which to judge the effectiveness of these measures is to evaluate their overall cost. Because the government relied so heavily on purchasing cooperation from business and labor, the eventual cost of the war was high.

How did these wartime activities affect the relationship between industrialists, workers, and the government? Before declaring war, Wilson worried mostly about the chance the war offered for industrialists to reverse the recent regulation of their business activities. 'War means autocracy...', Wilson told the Secretary of the Navy, Josephus Daniels. 'The people we have unhorsed will inevitably come into the control of the country, for we shall be dependant upon the steel, oil, and financial magnates. They will run the nation' [162 *p. 103*]. Wilson's prediction came to pass. By the end of the war, the old Progressive idea of punishing and regulating corporations gave way to a new faith in the 1920s that the government could build a cooperative, friendly alliance with business to protect the common good. To many disillusioned reformers, the new business–government relationship was a perversion of the original reform agenda [74; 159]. The government's failure to continue its wartime partnership with workers was also seen by many liberals as a missed opportunity to advance the cause of social justice in the United States.

DRAFTING AN ARMY

The idea of conscripting a mass, national army was a new one. Traditionally, Americans had fought their wars primarily with volunteers. What accounts for Wilson's decision to advocate a national draft? In part, Britain's experience illustrated the problems inherent in fighting a total war with volunteers. For two years, Britain watched its best and brightest march off to France with little thought of the consequences for the civilian economy. By 1916, Britain turned to conscription to apportion the talents in its population more rationally between military and civilian tasks. The reality of total war was that unrelenting civilian production was as important as fielding armies on the battlefield.

The pre-war preparedness movement helped make conscription ideologically more acceptable to Americans by emphasizing the virtues of military training for young men. Theodore Roosevelt, who was active in the preparedness movement, played a key role, convincing Wilson that the federal government would need to limit its use of volunteers. Fifty-eight years old, blind in one eye, the hero of the 1898 Spanish-American War was itching to lead a division to France. Roosevelt wanted to recapture the thrill of combat, and perhaps revive his political career. In early February 1917 Roosevelt wrote to Wilson and asked him for permission, in the event of war, to raise a division of volunteers. Newton Baker, the Secretary of War, wrote back and rejected his offer. In the meantime, Roosevelt obtained endorsements from the British and French governments so he wrote again, this time citing his heroic record in Cuba and his status as a retired Commander-in-Chief of the United States army. Baker sent the letter to Wilson who exclaimed, 'this is one of the most extraordinary documents I have ever read! Thank you for letting me undergo the discipline of temper involved in reading it in silence!' [97 *p. 138*]. Roosevelt would never fight in

France; instead, his four sons proudly donned uniforms. Archie Roosevelt was wounded and received the Croix de Guerre. His father told Clemenceau, 'I am prouder of his having received it than of my having been President!' [183 *p. 328*]. When the news arrived that his son Quentin had died in an aerial dogfight, Roosevelt was heartbroken but never wavered in his support for the war. 'It is very dreadful that [Quentin] should have been killed,' Theodore Roosevelt wrote, 'it would have been worse if he had not gone' [185 *p. 513*].

During the Civil War, the country had a short, troubled experience with conscription. Learning from their past mistakes, the government prohibited conscripts from buying substitutes. Because the Progressive era had given rise to an obsession with efficiency, army officials found it easy to present conscription as a modern management technique designed to ensure that the country apportioned its manpower resources correctly. Calling the draft 'selective service' was intended to underscore that the men selected were an elite group, not conscripts the government was forcing to fight [97].

Provost Marshall General Enoch H. Crowder headed the selective service system throughout the war. Crowder created 4,647 draft boards to serve as 'buffers between the individual citizen and the Federal Government' to head off protests from states that the federal government was seizing too much power [82 *p. 176*]. Men registered with a local draft board composed of prominent citizens from the community. Those who refused to register risked seeing their names in the paper as draft-dodgers or being rounded up in one of the periodic slacker raids the government conducted during the war. Few men were willing to risk public ostracism or jail. When Baker drew the first eligible registration number out of a huge fish bowl on 20 July 1917, local boards had recorded the names of 10 million men between the ages of twenty-one and thirty. By the end of the war approximately 24 million men had registered. Conscripts ultimately accounted for 72 percent of the four million men in the American army during the war.

Selective service regulations were designed to ensure the smooth functioning of the civilian economy, but local communities used more than economic criteria to decide who went to war. Protecting the social order at home was important to community draft boards. The largest class of deferments, 43 percent of all registrants, went to married men who were the sole economic support of their dependents. The immediate justification was that the government wanted to avoid the burden of supporting multitudes of wives and children. Some local boards, however, bragged that they forced alcoholic or philandering husbands to take care of their wives and children by threatening to take away their draft exemptions. Unmarried men were eligible for industrial and agricultural deferments.

The Selective Service Act only provided for religious-based conscientious objection. The most famous conscientious objector of the war was Sergeant

Alvin C. York who, like 80 percent of drafted conscientious objectors, was persuaded to support the war. York had grown up hunting wild turkeys in the Tennessee Appalachian Mountains. 'Them there Greeks and Italians and even some of our own city boys ... missed everything but the sky', the expert marksman York noted after watching an 82nd Division target practice [107 *p. 18*]. York became the most decorated soldier of the war by single-handedly silencing thirty-five German machine guns, killing twenty Germans, taking 132 prisoners, and leading his ambushed patrol back into Allied lines on 8 October 1918. His feats were extraordinary for any war, but the chance for an individual to make a distinct mark in battle was particularly limited in this one. The 4,000 conscripts who refused to abandon their moral or religious opposition to the war were required to perform non-combatant service. Out of these, 2,700 balked at performing any type of war-related work and 500 were jailed [97].

The desire to use the nation's manpower efficiently did not end once local draft boards decided who to put in uniform. Civilian experts in the new fields of personnel management and psychology offered their services to help the army classify the professional skills and intelligence of the entire recruit population. Civilian experts working for the Committee on the Classification of Personnel believed they could help the army match the right man with the right job. This scientific approach was appealing, but collecting information on the individual skills of each soldier took so long that often by the time the Committee tabulated the results, recruits had long since departed overseas.

While personnel experts interviewed soldiers about their occupational skills, approximately 400 psychologists administered 1.7 million intelligence tests under the overall leadership of Robert M. Yerkes. A commemorative book on Camp Travis, Texas, sentimentally chronicled what certainly must have been a bizarre episode in a young soldier's military career. Using the experiences of two fictional characters, the author described their trip to an army camp building for intelligence testing. The conversation between John Thompson, a bookkeeper in civilian life, and Zeke Gray, the son of a tenant farmer, foreshadowed how the tests would influence their respective fates in the army:

> 'I thought they had chairs and tables in schools,' Zeke ventured.
> 'If the room was full of furniture, how do you think they would get all these men in here?' John countered. [103 *p. 236*]

After tabulation of the initial five-minute literacy test was completed, John was instructed to remain seated and complete the Alpha exam given to literate recruits. He eventually received an A score of superior intelligence and was assigned to an officer training camp. Zeke, who perhaps had never held a pencil before, was sent to take the pictorial exam developed for illiterates. Faring no better on this exam, he soon found himself being interviewed by the camp psychologist.

> 'What is foolish about this?' the examiner asked. 'A bicycle rider, after being thrown from his bicycle in an accident, struck his head against a stone and was instantly killed. They picked him up and carried him to the hospital, and they do not think he will get well again.'
> 'He should not have been riding so fast,' answered Zeke. [103 *p. 236*]

Wrong answer, according to the examiner's correction sheet. From a series of responses like these, the psychologist gave Zeke a D minus, which, in the jargon of the day, branded him a moron. According to the author of the story, Zeke was properly placed in a labor battalion.

This idealized illustration of the practical uses of intelligence testing resonates poorly with present-day readers whose attention focuses more on the ridiculous questions asked than on Zeke's inappropriate answers. Now-classic examples of the cultural biases inherent in these early exams are reprinted in Document 4. The testing protocol called for instructors to shout instructions in English and have soldiers change tasks every minute or so. The resulting intimidation and confusion no doubt caused many soldiers to score poorly [101].

Many army officials were skeptical about the usefulness of intelligence testing. 'I am not convinced that the stupid man, with proper training and leading, is necessarily going to give way in the trenches', wrote one officer [103 *p. 237*]. This officer made an important point since wartime psychologists never presented any direct evidence linking intelligence with performance on the battlefield. During the war, the army paid little attention to intelligence test results.

The public, however, became fascinated by this snapshot of the country's intellectual abilities. Intelligence tests enjoyed their greatest post-war success in public schools where more sophisticated versions are still routinely used to measure student aptitude [75]. Test results released after the war purported to show that the average white American soldier had a mental age of thirteen. Widely reported figures claimed that average mental age was 11.01 for Italians, 11.34 for Russians, 10.74 for Poles, and 10.41 for American-born blacks. Overall, a whopping 80 percent of African-Americans scored poorly enough to be considered feeble-minded. The geographical distribution of scores indicated that Western and Northern states held more intelligent people than the Southern states. Some commentators criticized the tests, but many others accepted data about the low intelligence of African-Americans and eastern European immigrants because it provided comforting evidence that the established racial hierarchy was scientifically valid [101].

The truth was that the tests measured level of education, economic background, and familiarity with mainstream American culture. The results revealed the dismal state of formal education in America. Twenty-five percent of the soldier population was required to take the test for illiterates. The majority of native-born white men had completed only seven years of school, while foreign-born and Southern black men averaged 4.7 years and 2.6 years of schooling respectively. When these figures were released, the Progressive-era campaign for mandatory schooling had just ended. In 1918, Mississippi became the final state in the nation to pass a compulsory school attendance law.

PAYING FOR THE WAR

Money was an important part of the American war effort. The total cost of the war was an overwhelming $35.5 billion. This meant the war cost $2 million an hour or 8.7 percent of the nation's estimated wealth [184]. Of this amount, $11.2 billion went to the Allies. Money well spent, according to Secretary of the Treasury McAdoo. 'The dollars that we sent through these loans to Europe were, in effect, substitutes for American soldiers, and the extent to which we were able to save the lives of the young men of America would be measured by the extent to which we could make operative, quickly and effectively, the credits the Allies needed to purchase supplies in American markets,' he wrote in his memoirs [10 *pp. 376–7*]. Wilson had another reason for supporting Treasury loans to the Allies. 'England and France have not the same views with regards to peace that we have by any means,' Wilson told his advisor Colonel House in July 1917, 'when the war is over, we can force them to our way of thinking, because by that time they will be, among other things, financially in our hands ...' [178, vol. vii *p. 180*].

Besides saving American lives, boosting sales of American goods and perhaps influencing the peace, the government wanted Americans to use their money to connect personally with the war effort. 'Any great war must necessarily be a popular movement,' McAdoo noted, 'It is a kind of crusade; and like all crusades, it sweeps along on a powerful stream of romanticism' [10 *p. 374*]. McAdoo intended to tap into the patriotic mood which had settled over the country and entice Americans from all walks of life, 'business men, workmen, farmers, bankers, millionaires, school-teachers, laborers' to loan their dollars to the government in the form of liberty loans or war stamps [10 *p. 378*]. According to McAdoo, every person who bought a $50 liberty bond, a $5 war savings certificate, or a 25 cent thrift stamp felt personally connected to the war. Americans responded overwhelmingly to the request that they do their share and form a 'financial front' to support the men in the trenches. Overall, the loan campaigns raised $21.4 billion [184].

Document 5 is the reprint of a liberty bond poster. This poster illustrates the propaganda functions of war bond posters. Why refer to the German soldier as a Hun? The word Hun, written in red, links it to the red blood on the bayonet and on the soldiers' hands. The Huns were a warlike people from Asia who invaded Europe in the fourth and fifth centuries to destroy the remnants of Roman civilization. Few Germans or Austrians were actually descended from them, but it was a label that stereotyped the Germans as depraved and uncivilized, rather than depicting them as part of a culture that had produced Mozart and Beethoven and sent millions of productive and respected immigrants to the United States. This poster also depicts the Germans as poised to invade across the Atlantic. While this fear was unrealistic, Americans were nervous enough about the patrolling of coastal areas by German U-Boats to respond to images like these as if the threat was indeed everywhere. This poster suggests that the individual act of buying a liberty bond could affect the outcome of the war, tapping into a traditional American belief in the power of the individual.

Liberty loan campaigns helped the civilian public connect personally to the war effort and they raised an enormous amount of revenue. But financing two-thirds of the war's cost through war bonds rather than taxation also caused inflation. Average people borrowed money to buy liberty bonds, richer ones used them as tax shelters, and banks bought bonds which they used as reserves for other loans. This meant that, paradoxically, bond drives actually put more money rather than less into the economy. During the war, the money supply increased 75 percent and the consumer price index doubled [75]. Borrowing the money from citizens during an inflationary period and then re-paying it later with deflated currency also increased the overall cost of the war to the government.

Taxes only paid for one-third of the war's total cost. The well-to-do assumed the largest tax burden. Tax rates in 1918 ranged from 3 percent for a taxable income of $2,000 to 70.3 percent for incomes over $1 million. Payments from the 77.7 percent of Americans who earned less than $3,000 only accounted for 3.6 percent of the income tax collected that year [82]. The Revenue Act of 1917 and 1918 continued the country's trend towards a progressive tax code which permanently shifted the major burden of financing the federal government from indirect consumption taxes like tariffs to direct taxes on incomes and profits [75]. Though the rich paid a disproportionate share of income tax, they were the prime collectors of future bond interest payments. Over 70 percent of bond purchases were made by Americans with incomes over $2,000 a year.

PROPAGANDA AND CIVIL LIBERTIES

On the eve of his war message Wilson sent for *New York World* reporter Frank Cobb, and anguished, 'to fight you must be brutal and ruthless, and the spirit of ruthless brutality will enter into the very fibre of our national life, infecting Congress, the courts, the policeman on the beat, the man in the street.' Wilson went on to predict that '... free speech and the right of assembly would go. He said a nation couldn't put its strength into a war and keep its head level; it had never been done' [178, vol. vi *pp. 506–7*]. Americans faced the difficult task of fighting a total war without adopting an 'ends justifies the means' approach towards curtailing freedom of speech. Many patriots argued that the United States needed the support of each citizen and that the nation had the right to protect itself from internal traitors and spies. Critics retorted that the victory would be a hollow one if America abandoned the very values it was fighting the war to extend world-wide.

In 1917 the intellectual, John Dewey, suggested that the war might give Progressives an opportunity to break 'the individualistic tradition' that prevailed in the country and give Americans a social conscience [75 *p. 50*]. Through supporting the war, Americans would become involved in philanthropic community activities and begin to appreciate the need for social reform. Randolph Bourne, a former student, replied that 'if the war is too strong for you to prevent, how is it going to be weak enough for you to control and mould to your liberal purpose?' [3 *p. 339*]. Many liberals, however, shared Dewey's faith that the war would improve American democracy by strengthening the individual's interest in the common good and creating an informed citizenry. Progressive reformers had perfected the tactic of using factually-based, emotional appeals to inform and interest the public in social justice [75]. Muckrakers (as advocacy journalists of the time were called) used written exposés on corruption, photographs of children, and melodramatic stories of working-class hardship to create a groundswell of support for social reform. Jacob Riis and Lewis Hines, for example, took posed photographs of barefoot children working in horrendous factory and sweatshop conditions. Their shocking images generated tremendous support for child labor laws. Technically, Riis and Hines were guilty of manipulating images to arouse emotions and win support for a good cause. Were these same techniques appropriate to create public support for the war?

Wilson appointed a prominent muckraker, George Creel, to head the Committee on Public Information (CPI). Creel in turn surrounded himself with other liberal journalists to inform the public about the war effort. The press received guidelines about what information was considered confidential, such as news of troop sailings and placing units in specific places. Creel delighted in pointing out that there was no need for censorship since the press voluntarily followed the CPI's reasonable guidelines [196]. The CPI published an official bulletin that detailed the government's daily activities, wrote press releases explaining complex issues and organized war expositions that ten million people attended. In keeping with their mission to educate the American people, the CPI recruited university scholars to design war course materials for all school levels. The Committee distributed its literature in foreign languages because the Americans it needed to reach were a mixed lot that had different concerns about the war. The CPI addressed Russian immigrants who had come to America to avoid conscripted military service, Irish-Americans who had little reason to support British imperial ambitions, minority ethnic groups from the Austro-Hungarian Empire who were more interested in fledgling independence movements in their native lands than German aggressions, and German-Americans who were unsure about fighting their own relatives.

The CPI prided itself on the enormous amount of factual information that it distributed to the press, but the agency added a distinct emotional edge to much of the material it provided for mass consumption. The CPI sponsored lectures by 'Four-Minute Men' who spoke before audiences at the movies, in markets, fairs, and churches. Their time was originally limited to four minutes because that was how long it took to change the reels for silent films. Numbering almost 75,000, Creel estimated the Four-Minute Men gave nearly seven million impassioned speeches during the war on topics such as German submarine warfare, the importance of freedom of the seas, German war practices, and German plots within the country to sabotage munition factories. By 1918, Four-Minute Men were also leading audiences through the singing of patriotic war songs to encourage direct participation over passive listening [195].

The theme of wartime unity ran through CPI literature and propaganda. The Committee produced one-reel propaganda films to publicize the contributions of marginalized groups. These films had titles such as 'The American Indian gets into the War Game' and 'Colored Americans – activities of the Negroes, both in the military forces and in war work at home'. CPI propaganda emphasized how immigrants and native-born Americans, labor and capital, farmers and workers were all working together to win the war.

There were numerous signs, however, that the growing passion for solidarity had opened a Pandora's box. Passionate patriots soon demanded 100 percent dedication to the war effort. German-Americans were the easiest to suspect of disloyalty in this charged atmosphere. After the war, Creel described the paranoia that gripped the country. 'Every fire, every explosion in a munition-plant, every accident on land or sea, was straightway credited to the "spy system," if the cut in a child's hand didn't heal quickly, then the "Germans" had put germs in all the court-plaster; ... if any woman's headache didn't yield to remedies, then the "Germans" had "doped" the particular pill or powder', he noted with dismay [196 *p. 170*].

Throughout the country, German-Americans went from being the most respected and desired immigrant group to the most hated [163]. Nearly half of the states banned or restricted the teaching of German because it was the language that disseminated the ideals of autocracy, brutality and hatred [197]. A hamburger became a liberty sandwich, sauerkraut became liberty cabbage, German measles was renamed liberty measles. Occasional mobs attacked German-Americans or businesses with German-sounding names. The most famous case of vigilante violence was the lynching of Robert Prager in Collinsville, Illinois in April 1918. Tensions were high in nearby Maryville because of rumors that an agent of the Kaiser was threatening to blow up the mine where Prager temporarily worked. No one in the mob realized that Prager had tried to enlist in the navy but had been rejected for medical reasons. But they did remember the sympathetic views towards Germany that this strange, argumentative man had held. These views had cost him his union membership and without it he could not work in the mines. Unwilling to accept this injustice, Prager posted a list of his grievances against union leaders and retreated to Collinsville. Angered by the audacity of this 'German spy' to challenge the union, a mob descended on Prager's house. The police intervened, put Prager in the town jail and closed all the saloons in town. The angry mob, however, overwhelmed the four policemen and mayor guarding the jail. When the first attempt to hang Prager failed, the mob granted his request to write a letter that they expected to name the others involved in the plot to blow up the mine. Instead, Prager wrote a letter to his mother and father who still lived in Dresden. 'Dear parents,' he wrote in German, 'I must on this fourth day of April, 1918, die. Please pray for me, my dear parents. This is my last letter and testament' [197 *p. 10*]. The national press condemned the lynching, but many of the atrocity stories they had printed of German soldiers raping Belgian women and bayoneting babies helped fan the flames of rage and hysteria.

Before the war, German saboteurs had attacked American munitions plants. The most spectacular incident occurred at a munitions depot in Black Tom, New Jersey on the Hudson River [62]. Citizens as far away as Philadelphia, Pennsylvania, heard the huge explosions. Shrapnel left holes in the Statue of Liberty and shock-waves shattered thousands of windows in the Lower Manhattan section of New York City. The press attributed the explosion to careless security guards who had lit fires to drive away mosquitos, and triggered a massive accident. The government, however, suspected and later proved that German spies had recruited German-Americans and British-hating Irish to blow up the armaments awaiting shipment to Britain. Once the country entered the war, therefore, there was a legitimate need to protect military and industrial installations from sabotage and to track the movements of suspected spies. During the course of the war, however, the government began to consider dissenting words as dangerous as treasonous acts. Was urging men to disobey the draft the same as blowing up a factory? Super-patriots answered that they were since both acts hampered the war effort and helped Germany. But when did the government stop defending citizens from legitimate threats and become itself an enemy of the people?

The CPI did not endorse censorship, but the Postmaster General did. In 1917, Postmaster General Albert Sidney Burleson refused to deliver the publications of pacifists and radicals. The Trading with the Enemies Act in 1917 required that all foreign-language publications submit English-language translations of articles about the war. Excerpts from the Espionage Act of 1917 and the Sedition Act of 1918 are reprinted in Document 5. Consider the wide range of activities the Acts covered and the broad powers they gave to the government. Which clauses are understandable in time of war, and which ones threaten basic civil liberties? The most famous American convicted of violating the Espionage Act was Eugene Debs, leader of the Socialist Party and a perennial candidate for President. When he began his speech in Canton, Ohio, on 15 June 1918, Debs was aware of the risk he was taking in delivering his anti-war message. He noted that '... it is extremely dangerous to exercise the constitutional right of free speech in a country fighting to make democracy safe in the world. (Applause)' [6 *p. 417*]. Instead of caution, however, Debs went on to describe the war as nothing more than a capitalist rivalry for international markets and raw materials. 'The master class has always declared the wars; the subject class has always fought the battles. The master class has had all to gain and nothing to lose, while the subject class has had nothing to gain and all to lose – especially their lives,' he shouted [6 *p. 425*]. To Debs, the Germans were not the true enemy of working-class Americans.

> In passing, I suggest that we stop a moment to think about the term 'landlord.' 'LANDLORD!' Lord of the Land! The Lord of the land is indeed a super-patriot. This lord who practically owns the earth tells you that we are fighting this war to make the world safe for democracy – he, who shuts out all humanity from his private domain; he who profiteers at the expense of the people who have been slain and mutilated by multiplied thousands, under pretense of being the great American patriot. It is he, this identical patriot who is in fact the arch-enemy of the people; it is he that you need to wipe from power. It is he who is a far greater menace to your liberty and your well-being than the Prussian junkers on the other side of the Atlantic Ocean (Applause). [6 *p. 430*]

For this speech Debs was arrested and sentenced to ten years in prison for violating the terms of the Espionage Act.

Which aspects of this speech violate the law? The answer from the Supreme Court was that the speech failed the 'clear and present danger' test. The criterion for this test was established in *Schenck versus U.S.* in March 1919. 'The question in every case is whether the words used are used in such circumstances and are of such a nature as to create a clear and present danger that they will bring about the substantive evils that Congress has a right to prevent', wrote Supreme Court Justice Oliver Wendell Holmes, Jr. in a decision that upheld the conviction of Charles T. Schenck for writing and mailing pamphlets urging men to avoid the draft. 'It is a question of proximity and degree', Holmes continued. 'When the nation is at war many things that might be said in time of peace are such a hindrance to its efforts that their utterance will not be endured so long as men fight and that no Court could regard them as protected by a constitutional right' [201 *p. 32*]. Was opposing the war like yelling fire in a crowded movie theater? How could anyone speak out against the war if dissent posed a clear and present danger to national security? This Supreme Court decision introduced significant legal restrictions on the right of free speech during time of war by making the circumstances in which dissent was uttered as important as the words themselves [199]. The speaker now became responsible for the reactions of listeners and the probable consequences of his or her utterances. This remained the standard used to enforce the Espionage Act until 1944 when the Court required the government to show that the speaker had specific intent to hamper the war effort.

In 1920, Debs once again ran for President from his jail cell and the martyred radical received one million votes. President Warren Harding finally pardoned him in 1921. Despite the jailing of their leader, the Socialist Party survived the war. Another radical group, the Industrial Workers of the World (IWW), was not as fortunate. The IWW organized the exploited workers who labored in lumber camps, mines, and migrant camps. The anti-war IWW never recovered from the blow of their entire leadership receiving long prison terms for violating the Espionage and Sedition Acts [68].

The excesses of war hysteria revealed an ugly, brutal side of American society that strained the earlier optimism that the war would strengthen the nation's democratic impulses. The government had not met the challenge of protecting civil liberties as it mobilized all the country's physical and emotional resources to fight a total war. Total war demanded not only that the country channel its raw materials, re-tool its factories, and conscript an army. It also demanded that the American people think as one. This was perhaps the greatest threat that total war posed to the future of American democracy.

CHAPTER THREE

SOCIAL CHANGES AT HOME: PROGRESSIVISM RUNS ITS COURSE

The abridgement of civil liberties was a major failing of American democratic impulses during the war. Progressive reformers, however, did register some key successes. Their most significant accomplishments were two amendments to the Constitution, one prohibiting the manufacture of alcoholic beverages and the other granting women the right to vote. African-Americans relied less on legislation to improve their lives, and more on their own initiative. The booming war economy offered many African-Americans the chance to leave the South and migrate to the North to take factory jobs. The most historic development on the domestic front, however, concerned the fates of immigrants. After the war, the United States shut its doors, thus ending the massive flow of talent and ambition from overseas that had defined America as the land of opportunity. Why did the war result in the extension of rights to some and the denial of opportunity to others? How did the war become a force that propelled social change in the United States? This chapter will address these key questions.

PROHIBITION

The war gave temperance reformers the opportunity to link their crusade against alcohol to nationwide concern that a whole generation of young men was about to be corrupted by the military. Responding to concern that army life would expose clean-cut young men to the drunkenness and prostitution associated with the hard and fun-loving life of a soldier, Wilson created the Commission of Training Camp Activities (CTCA) and appointed Raymond Fosdick, a civilian reformer, to head it [154; 160]. Acting on powers granted to him in the Selective Service Act, Wilson outlawed prostitution in broad zones around domestic training camps. The CTCA waged an all-out campaign to protect the morals of young soldiers and rid the military of venereal disease since this affliction immediately rendered a soldier unfit for overseas duty. Their sex education programs vividly introduced soldiers to the horrors

of venereal disease and made available a reasonably effective chemical pro-
phylaxis treatment. 'Damaged Goods' was a film shown to soldiers to
convey the horror of syphilis and the foolishness of trusting cures by 'quack'
doctors. The film recounted the sad tale of a man, unhappy at the prospect
of an arranged marriage, who becomes drunk at his bachelor party and ends
up in the arms of a 'girl of the streets'. The man not only contracts venereal
disease, but he buys an ineffective cure from a disreputable doctor and gives
the disease to his innocent wife and child. One psychologist observed a
group of soldiers' reaction to the film, and noted its weaknesses. 'When men
make remarks concerning the "Girl in the Streets" such as "That would
make a man catch somethin'" ... "By God, Some Stuff" ... "Go to it boy" ...
they are not at the same time susceptible to social hygiene instruction,' the
psychologist contended [103 *p. 238*]. On the other hand, he conceded that
the graphic depiction of venereal sores had the desired effect. The erring
youth's 'investigation of his own condition evidently went home to many of
them ... the hospital scenes silenced them all,' the psychologist reported with
satisfaction. This frank discussion of sexual intercourse and venereal disease
was not in the reformers' eyes a license for illicit sex. As a substitute, they
organized athletic and educational activities within the training camps to
consume soldiers' free time and pent-up sexual energy. But the CTCA's first
goal was to keep soldiers fit for service, and these reformers knew that some
soldiers would find a way to enjoy female companionship. In this respect,
the CTCA rendered a valuable military service by providing a practical way
to keep the venereal disease rate at an all-time low in the wartime army
[160].

By the end of the First World War, however, the CTCA had managed to
offend many local groups. Churches considered the sex education films
pornographic. The CTCA had organized Sunday entertainment for soldiers
in violation of local statutes and ignored arguments from some community
leaders that shutting down regulated houses of prostitution simply pushed
prostitutes on to the streets. A member of the San Francisco Board of Super-
visors expressed the feelings of many towns across the country when he
proclaimed '... that nobody had the right to come to San Francisco and dic-
tate to the San Francisco people what the social life of their city should be'
[154 *p. 194*]. At the end of the war, therefore, most communities ignored the
sample anti-vice laws which departing CTCA officials encouraged them to
enact to rid their cities permanently of prostitution.

The backlash against prohibition took longer to develop. Prohibition
began as a temporary wartime measure to protect the morals of soldiers and
to save grain. The Selective Service Act forbade the sale of liquor to men in
uniform and in August 1917, the Lever Food and Fuel Control Act forbade
the use of foodstuffs to distill liquor. Prohibition was destined, however, to
become a permanent way of life.

The temperance movement was already quite popular when the United States entered the war. By 1917, twenty-six states were dry and over half the people in the country lived in areas or states that prohibited alcohol. Since the turn of the century, the Anti-Saloon League and the Women's Christian Temperance Movement had made a series of religious, scientific, moral, and economic arguments against alcohol [167]. Churches were in the front lines of the temperance movement, motivated by their conviction that drink destroyed the self-discipline and morality required for salvation. Changing medical evidence bolstered the temperance cause as well. Prior to 1860, alcohol was popularly regarded as a stimulant and was used by manual workers to enhance physical activity, to warm them when they worked outside, and was drunk on the advice of doctors for heart conditions. Medical experimentation soon revealed that alcohol was a depressant which clouded judgement and impaired physical performance. Habitual and excessive use, researchers discovered, turned alcohol into a poison which destroyed the liver, damaged unborn children and caused insanity. Once workingmen's compensation laws began holding employers liable for industrial accidents after 1908, factory owners had additional economic incentive to restrict alcohol consumption at work.

Temperance propagandists also drew a link between strong drink and crime. Prostitution, gambling, and saloons went hand in hand in many cities. In a 1918 issue of *Collier's Weekly*, reporter Will Irwin described the tragic chain of events likely to follow a black man's purchase of a gin bottle with the picture of a naked white woman on it. After consuming the product, Irwin wrote, the man '... sits in the road or in the alley at the height of his debauch, looking at that obscene picture of a white woman on the label, drinking in the invitation which it carries. And then comes opportunity. There follows the hideous episode of the rope or the stake' [*167 p. 121*]. Rape was just one consequence of alcohol for women. Liquor, the Reverend Mark A. Matthews warned, transformed the good, loving husband 'into a heartless wretch, and makes him steal the shoes from his starving babe's feet to find the price for a glass of liquor' [*157 p. 66*].

During the war, there were new arguments to make in support of prohibition. The importance of each man working to his full potential strengthened the temperance cause. Senator James Wadsworth, however, thought it unfair to tell exhausted workers at the end of the day 'you shall not have a glass of beer' [*82 p. 98*]. The opposition of German-Americans to prohibition made temperance a patriotic cause to support. 'German brewers in this country have rendered thousands of men inefficient and are thus crippling the Republic in its war on Prussian militarism', the Anti-Saloon League declared [*167 p. 179*]. 'We have German enemies in this country too. And the worst of all our German enemies, the most treacherous, the most menacing are Pabst, Schlitz, Blatz, and Miller', proclaimed another temperance advocate [167 *p. 179*]. A poster exhibited by the Ohio Dry Federation was even more straightforward. It showed a soldier in the trenches, and asked 'Will *You* Back Me – Or Back Booze?' [164 *p. 114g*].

On 18 December 1918, Congress sent the Eighteenth Amendment to the states for ratification. When the Eighteenth Amendment took effect on 16 January 1920 only Rhode Island, New Jersey, and Connecticut had rejected it. Consumption of alcohol was halved during the nation's dry years, but Americans concluded that prohibition had failed. Organized crime syndicates ran profitable bootlegging operations and speakeasies became glamourous [164]. Instead of ridding alcohol from society, Americans concluded that they had passed an unenforceable law that generated disrespect for the law and made it socially acceptable, and for some social groups almost mandatory, to break the law. National prohibition ended in 1933 with the passage of the Twenty-first Amendment.

The lessons from this experience continue to resonate in American society in debates about the legalization of drugs, the abolition of hand guns, the regulation of pornography, and the imposition of age limits for purchases of alcohol. History may be repeating itself on college campuses across the nation where students often begin to drink well before reaching the legal drinking age of twenty-one. Whether or not the government has the right, responsibility or ability to control these activities is a question that still divides Americans.

FEMALE SUFFRAGE

'The executive tasks of this war rest upon me,' Wilson told the Senate on 30 September 1918. 'I ask that you lighten them and place in my hands instruments ... which I do not now have, which I sorely need, and which I have daily to apologize for not being able to employ' [169 *p. 3*]. Wilson was not making a plea for enhanced presidential powers, but for female suffrage. The President was responding to requests from the National American Woman Suffrage Association (NAWSA) that the nation thank women for supporting the war by giving them the right to vote. Wilson hoped his support for a female suffrage amendment to the Constitution would end picketing by militants from the National Women's Party who for months had stood outside the White House with banners asking 'how long must women wait for liberty?' [173 *p. 282*]. Arrests had not helped, as stories leaked out of forced prison feedings to end suffragist hunger strikes. The female militants thanked Wilson for his pardon by burning him in effigy before the White House and they resumed their silent vigil [82].

The Senate, however, defeated the female suffrage measure the next day and the fate of the suffrage amendment remained uncertain throughout the war. In 1917, eleven states allowed women to vote. Advocates argued that in time of war female suffrage was an issue for the federal, rather than state, government to decide. It was nine more months before Congress approved the Nineteenth Amendment. Final ratification from the states came on 26 August 1920.

During the period of neutrality, many suffragist leaders were active in the peace movement. They argued that giving women the vote would inject a more humane approach to world affairs. 'Women all the world over, speaking broadly, have one passion and one vocation, and that is the creation and preservation of life,' the British suffragist Emmeline Pethick-Lawrence declared in a speech to an American audience in 1914 [*5 pp. 47–8*]. A 1916 song entitled 'I Didn't Raise My Son to be a Soldier' popularized the notion that motherhood naturally led to pacifism. The lyrics, 'I brought him up to be my pride and joy. / Who dares to place a musket on his shoulder, / To shoot some other mother's boy', made the song a best-seller [*177 p. 11*].

Those who opposed female suffrage felt this peace activism illustrated exactly why giving women political power was foolhardy. Jane Addams, arguably the most famous and beloved woman in America because of her work with immigrants, experienced this wrath at firsthand. In 1915, Addams attended an international meeting of female peace activists held at The Hague in the Netherlands, where she joined a group charged with visiting neutral and belligerent countries to discuss the basis for a negotiated settlement. 'We heard in all countries similar statements in regard to the necessity for the use of stimulants before men would engage in bayonet charges – that they have a regular formula in Germany, that they give them rum in England and absinthe in France; that they have to give them "the dope" before the bayonet charge is possible,' she told a Carnegie Hall audience upon her return [*170 p. 226*]. Addams's suggestion that armies were drugging their soldiers to make them fight sent shock waves across the country. 'Jane Addams is a silly, vain, impertinent old maid, who may have done good charity work at Hull House, Chicago, but is now meddling with matters far beyond her capacity,' lambasted one journal [*170 p. 229*]. She was, the critics alternatively claimed, naive, foolish, unpatriotic, out of her depth, and most importantly, a perfect example of an interfering woman wreaking havoc in world affairs. The decision of the first woman elected to the House of Representatives, Jeannette Rankin, to join fifty-six male members and vote against the war resolution further confirmed to many skeptics that granting women the vote would force the country to accept 'peace at any price' as its foreign policy.

Since the turn of the century, the NAWSA had presented their demand for the vote strictly as a way to reinforce, rather than reject, the traditional desire of women to protect their families [*174*]. If mothers wanted to keep their families healthy and safe, they needed the ability to press for government inspections of meat, fire-safe building codes, regular garbage collections and temperance laws. A good family required both a male and female component, suffragists argued, and so did the government. 'City house-keeping has failed partly because women, the traditional housekeepers, have not been consulted as to its multiform activities,' Addams declared at the 1906 NAWSA convention [172 *p. 154*]. The arguments linking female suffrage with reform, however, guaranteed strong opposition from the liquor industry, urban political machines, and Eastern industrial interests to female suffrage [173].

Once the United States entered the war, the NAWSA refined their previous arguments to reflect the new roles that women were expected to play. In wartime America, the pacifist mother who refused to send her son into the army was no longer acting on legitimate maternal instincts. Instead, she was a bad, over-protective, selfish mother who was preventing her son having the chance to become an independent, robust man by serving in the army. Pershing paid homage to the icon of the devoted mother who willingly sent her son off to war by urging overseas soldiers to send a card on Mother's Day. Over 1.4 million soldiers responded to his call [177]. Women actively supported the war effort in numerous ways. Sixteen thousand accompanied the AEF overseas as nurses, telephone operators or welfare workers working in army canteens [175]. Over eight million women volunteered for Red Cross work, producing millions of surgical dressings, sweaters, socks and mittens for soldiers and refugees [171]. Others temporarily moved into higher-paying factory jobs and government clerical positions. It is important to note, however, that this wartime work did not signal any permanent new opportunities for working women [169]. Women were essential to the war effort, the NAWSA argued, and deserved the vote as a reward for their past contributions and to guarantee their ongoing support.

The wartime environment also created new prejudices and fears which the NAWSA seized upon to advance their agenda. 'Every slacker has a vote. ... Every pro-German who can not be trusted with any kind of military or war service will have a vote,' NAWSA President Carrie Chapman Catt proclaimed. '... It is a risk, a danger to a country like ours to send 1,000,000 men out of the country who are loyal and not replace those men by the loyal votes of the women they have left at home' [82 *pp. 91–2*]. This was not the first time that the NAWSA used existing ethnic and racial prejudices to make its case. Before the war, suffragists suggested that white men needed the votes of white, native-born women to counter the growing numbers of immigrant voters and to ensure the future of white supremacy. This latter assertion, however, went unheeded by many Southern men. Of the ten states which refused to ratify the Nineteenth Amendment, nine were Southern states which feared that opening up the vote to women would inevitably lead to a re-evaluation of the Jim Crow laws that denied black men the vote [173].

AFRICAN-AMERICAN MIGRATION

The war seriously disrupted traditional sources of inexpensive immigrant labor at the exact moment that the demand for industrial goods was exploding. In 1914, 1.2 million immigrants entered the country. In 1917, only 110,618 arrived [22]. Labor recruiting agents soon turned to black Southerners to fill the void. Over half a million African-Americans migrated from the Southern farms and cities to the North, lured by offers of high-paying industrial jobs. Vivid descriptions of the social and political freedoms available in the North by black newspapers and letters from friends or relatives who made the trip convinced many to pack their bags. Ed Brown's description of the sharecropper's lot in the South illustrated the impossibility of getting ahead in a system which used credit and debt to tie farmers indefinitely to a specific patch of land. 'Along about April the bossman would say, "Ed is your cotton getting ready to chop?," by July when it is ready to pick, now the boss ask, "Is our cotton doing pretty good? ... " By the latter part of September it's picked ... Now Mr. Addison can handle it and just as sure as your livin he'll call it his'n. "My cotton, my corn, my crop"' [17 *p. 20*]. Paying off the lien on his crops taken to secure food or seed for the next year often consumed the sharecropper's portion of the cotton crop, leaving him dependent once again on credit or, even worse, still in debt.

For migrants, their new Northern life was filled with thrilling moments of realizing that they had escaped the Southern racial caste system. Industrial jobs gave working men and women cash in their pockets and freedom of movement. 'I can quit any time I want,' noted one migrant, without forfeiting a year's pay or losing his home as in the sharecropping system [18 *p. 261*]. Economic incentives also encouraged 400,000 white Southerners to head North in the 1920s, but they may not have shared black migrants' satisfaction in abandoning their regional racial customs [53]. One black migrant realized that in Chicago he did not need ' ... to look up to the white man, get off the street for him' [18 *p. 167*]. Another noticed that he was no longer afraid ' ... to rub up against a white person' accidentally on the street or sit down next to one on a streetcar [18 *p. 167*].

Middle-class Northern blacks worked through organizations like the Urban League and Young Men's Christian Association (YMCA) to help migrants adjust to the rhythms of industrial jobs and urban life. These groups served as mediators between the arriving black workforce and the white community. Their goals were to ensure that complaints about migrants' work habits did not close off opportunities for other black workers and that industrialists did not take advantage of the new arrivals' ignorance. Through these organizations, employers established baseball teams, glee clubs, and job-training programs for their black employees. The Urban

League and YMCA helped migrants find jobs and housing. They also offered continuous advice on how to adjust to their new environment. 'If you do well you will serve not only yourself but the entire race,' the Urban League reminded newcomers to Chicago [18 *p. 144*]. A list of dos and don'ts published by the *Chicago Defender*, a newspaper serving the African-American community, warned recent arrivals to watch their language, mind their manners, respect the law, keep their houses clean, send their children to school and not to '... abuse or violate the confidence of those who give you employment. Don't leave your job when you have a few dollars in your pocket' [18 *p. 146*].

The migratory wave of blacks northward continued into the immigrant-unfriendly 1920s, when one million more African-Americans made the trip. This steady influx from the South helped Harlem solidify its standing as the cultural mecca of the African-American community. Between 1919 and 1935, the years of the Harlem Renaissance, black writers, artists and musicians formed a legendary creative circle in New York City [22]. Industrial cities such as Chicago, Pittsburgh, Detroit, and Milwaukee also developed strong, thriving black communities.

Migrants, however, did not completely fulfill their dream of finding the 'promised land' in the North. Black workers were limited to semi-skilled positions in the industrial workplace and were relegated to segregated ghettos. Eventually, the gerrymandering of voting districts restricted their political influence. Industrialists often hired low-paid black workers to break strikes, occasionally triggering racial riots in those cities where an explosive combination of economic competition and racial hostility existed. African-Americans were more than willing to cross the picket lines of white unions which refused to admit them as members. The most serious wartime riot occurred in East St Louis in July 1917. Nine whites and thirty-nine blacks died, and hundreds were wounded. A subsequent Congressional investigation held white employers, labor leaders, and politicians responsible, but 6,000 African-Americans left the city anyway [24]. The Chicago racial riot of 1919 was another dismaying illustration that it was impossible to find a permanent haven from violent racial passions within American borders [25]. Yet the Chicago riot did portray some important differences between Northern and Southern race relations. The *Chicago Defender* reported with pride how blacks fought back against attacks from whites. Similar militancy in the South certainly would have led to the eventual tracking down and lynching of the black combatants. Instead, in the aftermath of the riot, Chicago collectively lamented the explosion of racial hatred and tried to forget the riot as quickly as possible [18].

THE FIRST RED SCARE AND IMMIGRATION RESTRICTIONS

Before the war, America was a country that welcomed millions to its shores each year. After the war, it begrudgingly accepted 150,000 immigrants a year. Wartime questions about the loyalty of immigrants, the so-called hyphenated Americans, energized the movement to restrict immigration. Yet the battle against Germany did not alone explain why America adopted this new policy since, paradoxically, Germans received the largest national quota under the new post-war laws. Instead, the Russian revolution proved to be the critical wartime event which finally turned existing prejudices against certain ethnic groups into concrete legislation. German authoritarianism was crushed by the war, but the struggle between communism and capitalism was just beginning in 1919 [194]. When anti-war hysteria about German sabotage gave way to concern that immigrants were importing radical bolshevik ideas to virgin American soil, the result was a wave of restrictive immigration legislation.

The ability of immigrants to assimilate was not a new concern when the United States entered the war, but the war provided a new twist by linking assimilation to national security. One-third of the country's immigrant population came from America's new enemies [163]. The sight of immigrants clinging to the ways of the Old World triggered extensive criticism from super-patriots. 'The passion for meddling in other people's business,' George Creel noted, was the distinguishing mark of crusaders for 100 percent Americanism. After the war, Creel related the following story of a visit to an immigrant home to illustrate their misplaced missionary zeal [196 *p. 166*]. The scene, he recalled, was

> The humble tenement home of a Bohemian family in Chicago during the first summer of the war.
>
> 'We are here,' the spokesman announced, impressively, 'in the interests of Americanization.'
>
> 'I'm sorry,' faltered the woman of the house, 'but you'll have to come back next week.'
>
> 'What!' The cry was a choice compound of protest and reproach. 'You mean that you have no *time* for our message! That you want to put *off* your entrance into American *life?*'
>
> 'No, no!' The poor Bohemian woman fell straightway into a panic, for not even a policeman has the austere authoritativeness of those who elect themselves to be light-bringers. 'We're *perfectly* willing to be Americanized. Why, we never turn *any* of them away. But there's nobody home but me. All the boys volunteered, my man's working on munitions, and all the rest are out selling Liberty Bonds. I don't want you to get mad, but *can't* you come back next week?' [196 *p. 166*]

It was entirely reasonable to assume, as Creel did, that since the war had concluded successfully without any crippling examples of immigrant disloyalty and numerous examples of enthusiastic immigrant participation, the campaign for 100 percent Americanism would become a footnote in history with little more to its credit than introducing a literacy test for adult immigrants in 1917. But in 1919, the new menace of bolshevism fortified the demand to restrict immigration.

It seemed to many that the country was coming apart in 1919. During this unstable period of strikes, recession, and escalating racial violence, it was a shock to learn that the Post Office had discovered thirty-four bombs addressed to prominent Americans [200]. Post Office clerk Charles Kaplan was reading a newspaper account of two mail bomb attacks on a subway ride home when he realized that the description of the packages matched that of sixteen packages he had recently set aside for insufficient postage. Kaplan's discovery triggered a nationwide investigation that netted eighteen more packages. In this highly-charged atmosphere, terrorists exploded dynamite outside the home of Attorney General A. Palmer Mitchell, the man heading the Justice Department's hunt for bolshevik terrorists. These attacks gave credibility to Mitchell's claim before a House committee that 'on a certain day which we have been advised of' radicals were planning 'to rise up and destroy the Government at one fell swoop' [194 *p. 105*]. In response to this perceived revolutionary threat, Mitchell raided the homes and offices of suspected radicals and deported a few hundred aliens with ties to radical organizations.

Just as there was some truth behind fears of German-orchestrated sabotage during the war, some American communists and strikers in 1919 were indeed recent immigrants interested in sparking an anti-capitalist revolution. More generally, however, poor working conditions in American factories, mines, and lumbering camps were responsible for the wave of strikes that traversed the country during the 1919 recession. As Palmer's presidential ambitions became more widely publicized and 1 May 1920 passed without the general revolution that he predicted, his influence and the fear of a domestic revolution diminished [75].

The First Red Scare was limited, but it was not without long-lasting effects. It was increasingly difficult to be either a radical or an immigrant in America. Coming on the heels of prosecutions under the Espionage and Sedition Acts, many radical organizations never recovered from government harassment during the Red Scare. The Red Scare also convinced many Americans that unchecked immigration threatened their economic, cultural, and political institutions.

Assumptions about the racial superiority of northern European races influenced the national quotas established by immigration laws in the 1920s. The National Origins Act of 1924 limited the number of European immigrants to 150,000 and allotted spots to European countries by computing a 2 percent quota based on the national origins of immigrants recorded in the 1890 census. By 1900, massive numbers of immigrants from eastern and southern European countries were making their way to the United States. Basing quotas on 1890 immigration patterns, therefore, ensured that a high percentage of future immigrants would come from respected countries like Germany, England and France rather than Italy, Russia or Poland [163]. Mexican and Canadian immigrants were exempt from quotas, but Asians were barred completely from entering the country. In 1929, the basis for determining quotas was changed to a 1920 census of the national origins of the American people, but the resulting quotas were the same.

Ironically, therefore, Americans overcame their fear of a bolshevik uprising by creating a revolutionary movement of their own. As historian John Higham notes, 'the country would never be the same again ... the vast folk movements that had formed one of the most fundamental social forces in American history had been brought to an end' [163 *p. 330*] The move of African-Americans to the North, the extension of the right to vote to women, and the enactment of national prohibition rounded out the series of radical changes American society underwent during the war.

CHAPTER FOUR

FIGHTING THE WAR

In 1914, a stalemate was reached on the western front. At first, soldiers tried to apply some of the old rules of chivalry to the new trench warfare. One striking example of this desire to fight a civilized war came during a moment known as the Christmas truce of 1914. On Christmas Day, British and German troops climbed out of the trenches and met on the desolate stretch of land called No Man's Land to sing carols and exchange small gifts of food and tobacco. At midnight, they resumed fighting. In 1915, however, officials of both armies took steps to ensure that this event was not repeated by ordering massive bombardments on Christmas Day.

Mass slaughter was the best characterization of the first three years of fighting on the western front [Map 3]. Generals on both sides adopted a strategy of attrition, resigning themselves to the fact that the enemy would not succumb until he was 'bled white'. In 1916, the Germans launched their great offensive at Verdun and the British attacked along the Somme River by hurling millions of men and bombs against the enemy. Each effort failed. A visit to Verdun starkly illustrates the human cost of this ten-month battle. The city itself had more symbolic than strategic value. It held one of the last forts to fall in the Franco-Prussian War of 1870 and the German strategists believed that the French determination to defend it at all costs would cause five Frenchmen to fall for every two Germans. The ensuing slaughter is evident today in the huge ossuary at Douaumont which houses the bones of the hundreds of thousands of unknown soldiers who died in the battle. In the end, the battle of Verdun weakened both sides [55; 60]. It was impossible for Germany to attack France so continuously without also paying a heavy cost itself. On the Somme, the British orchestrated a similarly massive assault on the German line with no success. The casualties again were staggering. Nineteen thousand British soldiers died on the first day of the offensive. By the time the battle ended four and a half months later over 400,000 British soldiers, 200,000 French soldiers, and 650,000 German soldiers were dead or wounded. Who won the battle? The British poet Edmund Blunden supplied the answer: 'The War had won, and would go on winning' [58 p. 1063].

Undeterred by the examples of these earlier disastrous offensives, the new French Commander-in-Chief, General Robert Nivelle, ordered a massive offensive at Chemin des Dames on 16 April 1917. This attack ended in disaster and mutiny. Morale in the French army reached a new low. General Henri Philippe Pétain replaced Nivelle, and restored order in his army by shooting some mutineers, granting soldiers long-delayed leaves home and deciding to wait for the Americans to arrive in force before launching another major offensive.

These previous examples of slaughter in the Allied armies gave the American Commander, General John J. Pershing, little incentive to turn his fresh troops over to Allied generals to command [191]. Instead, Pershing decided to create an independent American army. Only time would tell if this was a wise decision. But even an independent American army had to co-ordinate and compromise with the French and British. These compromises with the Allies influenced how, where, and when the American military fought.

Politicians, generals and soldiers leave a battle with different perspectives of what transpired. The politicians focus on how the fighting advanced the political goals of the war, the generals consider the overall strategic gains or losses, while soldiers remember the terrifying moments of confronting death at firsthand. This chapter will explore these differing perspectives, and evaluate how much American soldiers contributed to the eventual Allied victory in 1918.

LEADERSHIP AND STRATEGY

The steady call from Allied leaders for America to amalgamate its troops into already-formed French and British units was understandable given the seriousness of the situation along the western front. Besides mutiny in the French army and failed British offensives, Russia signed a separate peace with Germany on 3 March 1918. Pershing alone had the power to decide whether or not to form an independent army. When Pershing left the United States, Secretary of War Baker told him, 'I will give you only two orders – one to go to France and the other to come home. In the meantime your authority in France will be supreme' [115 *p. 12*].

There were political and strategic reasons for Pershing's refusal to turn his troops over to Allied commanders. Pershing was certain that amalgamation was politically impossible since the American people would never accept sending their sons into battle under a foreign flag. His insistence on creating an independent army also was in keeping with Wilson's desire to use a distinct American military contribution to justify a strong American voice in the peace settlement. Finally, Pershing had enormous faith in the ability of Americans, who had not experienced the demoralizing effects of attritional warfare, to break the stalemate along the western front by pur-suing a strategy that he called open warfare.

On the surface, the idea of open warfare seemed hopelessly naive. It called for the Americans to somehow draw the Germans out into the open battlefield and defeat them. Yet Pershing's emphasis on the performance of infantrymen, not artillery, was not as farfetched as it sounded at first. The elements of open warfare which Pershing identified as the most important – individual and line commander initiative in battle, using ground cover to advance, irregular formations, and rifle power – were used by the Germans in March 1918 to create the first major break in the trench lines since 1914 [Map 3]. The Germans knew that they needed to strike the fatal blow before the Americans established their independent army. Estimating (as the Americans did) that it would take two years before the United States could make a difference in the field, the Germans counted on the continuation of unconditional submarine warfare and an all-out assault in the spring of 1918 to win the war before Christmas [190].

The Germans took immediate advantage of their peace with Russia and transferred over one million men from the eastern front. These numbers gave them numerical supremacy on the western front for the first time since Verdun. Yet the break-through the Germans accomplished was not based on numbers alone. Many commanders had squandered such an advantage before by believing foolishly that frontal assaults by waves of men would cause the opposing line to crumble. These frontal attacks often succeeded in taking the opposing front-line trench because enemy troops retreated to second, third, and fourth reserve trenches. Exhausted from the effort of crossing No Man's Land, the attacking troops could not fend off counter-offensives from these reserve trenches and were soon pushed back to their own trench lines. In the March offensives the Germans limited their use of a heavy artillery bombardment to open the attack. They realized that the several days of massive bombing that both sides had used to weaken the enemy simply warned the other side that an attack was coming and created huge craters in No Man's Land for troops to cross. This time, small infantry teams advanced under artillery cover, got past strongly-defended front lines, then poured men through the opening to assault weak rear defenses and encircle Allied lines before front-line troops had time to fall back [63; 98].

The Americans did not initiate the new phase of open warfare, but they played a critical role in stopping the German drive towards Paris. On 28 March 1918, Pershing went to Marshal Ferdinand Foch, the newly appointed Supreme Commander of the Allied Armies on the western front. Temporarily putting his goal of an independent American army aside, Pershing told Foch that in the light of the seriousness of the situation, '... all that we have is yours; use them as you wish' [190 *p. 101*]. For two months American troops occupied quiet sectors so veteran French troops could join the active fighting. Finally, on 28–31 May troops from the 1st Division fought in the first offensive American action of the war at Cantigny where they seized a plateau at the Germans' farthest point of penetration to improve Allied observation of the enemy and positioning for future offensives [109]. Though successful, this first battle shattered any illusions that the American task would be easy. After the battle, Colonel Hansen Ely recalled, exhausted troops from the 28th Infantry 'could only stagger back, hollow-eyed with sunken cheeks, and if one stopped for a moment he would fall asleep' [190 *p. 128*].

The initiative on the battlefield still remained with the German army. The day before the Cantigny assault, the Germans began another offensive in Chemin des Dames. Within five days, the Germans advanced thirty miles to the Marne River, only forty miles from Paris. The Germans captured 50,000 prisoners and in panic one million people fled Paris. The 2nd Division played a crucial role in halting the German drive towards Paris at Chateau-Thierry by re-capturing Belleau Wood and Vaux. 'The marines didn't "win the war" here,' General Robert L. Bullard wrote later, '*But they saved the Allies from defeat*. Had they arrived a few hours later I think that would have been the beginning of the end: France could not have stood the loss of Paris' [4 *p. 39*]. The appearance of the Americans in battle at Cantigny and Chateau-Thierry provided a psychological boost for the Allied side and a corresponding fear in Germany that time was running out.

The Germans launched their fifth and last offensive at Rheims in July. Both sides felt that a critical turning point was at hand. 'If my blow at Rheims succeeds now, we have won the war,' German General Erich Ludendorff told an aide, not knowing that Foch simultaneously was warning 'if the German attack at Rheims succeeds we have lost the war' [115 *p. 82*]. After battling for five days, the German advance was halted by members of the 3rd, 26th, 28th, 42nd, and 93rd Divisions who fought alongside French troops in the Second Battle of the Marne. Rheims was battered, but remained under Allied control.

American reinforcements were beginning to make a mark, funneling fresh fighting troops into Allied armies just as the Germans had exhausted their reserves [9]. The German advance revealed the limited possibilities of open warfare when troops outran their supply lines and exhaustion took its toll. Ironically, the initial success of the spring offensives planted the seeds of defeat for the German army. German troops were now vulnerable to the counter-attacks that doomed all offensive actions on the western front.

A total of 140,000 American soldiers defended France against the German offensive, and close to 270,000 participated from 18 July–6 August in the Aisne–Marne counter-offensive [115]. The 1st and 2nd Divisions helped open the counter-offensive with the Battle of Soissons. Pershing considered this battle the real turning point in the war since the German army never regained the initiative. Six other American Divisions (3rd, 4th, 26th, 28th, 32nd and 42nd) suffered heavy losses in this joint French–American campaign to eliminate the Marne salient and open up the Paris–Chalons railway. Among the dead were the poet Joyce Kilmer and Quentin Roosevelt. When the British army routed German Divisions near Amiens on 8 August 1918, Ludendorff called it a 'black day' for the German army [98 *p. 248*]. The rout confirmed that the German spring offensives had failed. Bitter fighting was still ahead, however, as the 28th, 32nd, and 77th Divisions discovered in August while participating in the Oise–Aisne offensive with the French Sixth Army. This counter-offensive brought the Allies back in early September to the positions they had occupied when the German spring assault began.

During these counter-offensives, American Divisions fought under the command of the French and British. Some American Divisions remained attached to the British and French armies for the entire war. Hundreds of thousands of American soldiers, however, opened a new chapter in American military history on 12–16 September 1918 when they finally fought in an American sector under American generals. Close to 550,000 American soldiers (with 110,000 French troops lending mostly artillery and air support, and protecting the Americans' flanks) fought in the Battle of St Mihiel to reduce a salient held by the Germans since 1914[Map 3]. German troops had begun their assault on Verdun in 1916 from the salient, but now it was a quiet sector where both sides rested their troops. The Americans faced formidable defenses of barbed wire up to thirteen rows deep, elaborate trenches, and well-placed artillery and machine guns. This area was strategically important because it gave the enemy a jumping-off point for a flanking attack on Verdun or Nancy. Since June 1917 Pershing had wanted to attack St Mihiel, then drive towards Metz and win the war by penetrating the fortifications known as the Hindenburg Line* which protected the lateral railroad lines supplying the German army on the western front. By the time the Americans attacked the St Mihiel salient, pressing on to Metz was no longer an issue. Foch had limited the operation to flattening out the salient to prepare for a coordinated Allied assault set to begin on 26 September along the entire western front. The Americans were scheduled to fight first at St Mihiel, and again ten days later in the Meuse–Argonne campaign* when the general Allied offensive began.

The Americans attacked while the 23,000 German troops holding the salient were in the midst of withdrawing to a more fortified position. In the face of a retreating enemy, the Americans captured the railroad lines as far as Nancy. The 1st, 2nd, 4th, 5th, 26th, 42nd, 82nd, 89th, 90th Divisions took part in the offensive for the relatively light cost of 7,000 casualties. In retrospect, the lack of German resistance camouflaged numerous American errors during the attack. Deficiencies included lax discipline, commanders who were located too far back to control troop advances, long and confusing orders, and traffic jams which prevented supplies from reaching the front [113]. A German intelligence report summed up the American performance by noting 'the Americans have not yet sufficient experience and are accordingly not to be feared in a great offensive. Up until this time our men have had too high an opinion of the Americans...' [190 *p. 189*]. Adding to concerns about the future fighting abilities of the American army was Pershing's decision to use his most experienced combat divisions at St Mihiel. Pershing wanted to ensure victory in order to quiet his Allied critics who doubted the ability of American staff officers to conceive and lead their own offensive [115]. Pershing consequently entered the Meuse–Argonne campaign with his best troops resting in the rear and five of his nine divisions fighting for the first time.

The objective of the Meuse–Argonne offensive was to break through German fortifications and converge with British and French assaults further west to disrupt the railroad between Lille and Thionville. This critical railroad line sent 250 supply trains a day to the German army in the north of France. Foch believed that losing this vital supply line in the midst of defending against four, concurrent Allied offensives from the North Sea to the Meuse River would force the Germans to retreat and move the fighting on to German soil [Map 3]. On the opening day of the battle, 600,000 American troops faced five weak, but well-placed German Divisions who quickly called on fifteen nearby reserve Divisions for help. The challenging goal was to advance over the narrow terrain between the hilly, densely-wooded Argonne Forest on the west and the heights of the unfordable Meuse River on the east. In the center a 13-mile long and 20-mile wide tunnel-like stretch of land gave the Germans a third entrenchment on high ground [96; 110; 115].

The Germans had used their four-year occupation to create an impregnable fortress of man-made defenses to enhance the favorable terrain. The Germans named their defense lines (*Stellung*) after witches in a Wagnerian opera – Giselher, Kriemhilde, and Freya [96]. It took the inexperienced Americans four days, instead of the anticipated two, to reach the Kriemhilde Stellung, the strongest line of German fortifications. The assault temporarily halted there, amid what a British observer called the worst traffic jam of the war. On 4 October, Pershing resumed the offensive, replacing the no longer inexperienced 35th, 37th, 79th and 91st Divisions with the battle-tested 1st, 3rd, and 32nd Divisions. Pershing understood that without seizing the high ground east of the Meuse and in the Argonne Forest, his army could not advance. Despite valiant assaults for six days, the Germans stayed put along the Kriemhilde Stellung and the Meuse–Argonne offensive had now taken on the character of previous western front battles. The Americans tried to kill as many of the enemy as possible while contesting small, well-defended plots of ground.

This battle of attrition in the American sector contradicted Pershing's avowed preference for open warfare, but he angrily denounced accusations from Foch that inept American leadership was preventing American troops from keeping up with the advancing French and British armies. With some justification, Pershing noted that the heavy German reinforcements sent to fight in the American sector (which was now 21 percent of the western front) weakened other parts of the line and made the French and British break-throughs possible. Foch also had contributed to the logistical woes of the American army by giving the Americans little time to plan their Meuse–Argonne campaign. Yet Pershing had accepted the assignment and he now needed to fulfill it or risk undermining Allied faith in his independent American army.

On 14th October, the 3rd, 4th, 5th, 32nd, 42nd, 77th, and 82nd Divisions renewed the Meuse–Argonne offensive and finally, the 32nd and 42nd Divisions made a limited dent in the Kriemhilde Stellung. It had taken three weeks to meet the campaign's original first-day objective. Pershing now divided his growing force into two field armies. As the First Army regrouped under its new commander, Major General Hunter Liggett, it began tactical training of infantry assault teams to knock out the machine-gun nests that hampered the advance of the infantry. These units performed well when the Americans (the 2nd, 5th, 77th, 78th, 80th, 89th, 90th) resumed their offensive on 1 November 1918. Infantry–artillery coordination improved, commanders became confident enough to approve night attacks, and aerial bombing and mustard gas attacks supported infantry troops' advance. The Americans were finally fighting a war of movement, but only after the attritional-style of warfare had exhausted their enemy's manpower and supplies. In pursuit of a withdrawing German army, the First Army reached Sedan and the Second Army was beginning a drive towards Metz when the Armistice came into effect on 11 November 1918 [113]. Overall, the Americans advanced thirty-four miles during the campaign.

When the war ended the AEF counted 255,970 battle casualties, including 50,280 killed [2]. The crowning achievement of the American army was the immense effort exerted during the forty-seven-day Meuse–Argonne campaign. Nearly 1.2 million soldiers (850,000 of whom were combatant troops) fought in the battle, more soldiers than the entire Confederate army during the Civil War [96; 110]. Other wars have their horrific days, such as Antietam during the Civil War and the D-Day landings during the Second World War, that portray in starkly dramatic terms the horror of combat and the immensity of the battle. Yet, because American battle deaths paled in comparison to those of France (1.3 million), Britain (900,000), Germany (1.6 million), and Russia (1.7 million), the Americans are often portrayed as 'barely bloodied' by the war [2]. This is a gross distortion of the reality of fighting in an historically unique and great battle. In the Meuse–Argonne offensive, casualty rates averaged 2,550 a day with 6,000 Americans dying each week. There was no stop and start as in previous great battles; instead, the psychological and physical horror was analogous to the continuous struggle waged during the jungle campaigns of the Second World War and the Vietnam War. Overall, 50,000 men died in what amounted to six months in battle – nearly as many as died in nine years of fighting in Vietnam and three years of fighting in Korea. 'Barely bloodied', therefore, is hardly an accurate description of the American army during the war.

Did this enormous effort contribute concretely to the Allied victory? The real architect of the Allied victory was Foch, who devised the final coordinated Allied blow against the German army. In a war which had a voracious appetite, the American material contribution was negligible. The Americans contributed few 75mm guns and no 155mm howitzers, no ammunition except shrapnel, hardly any tanks or airplanes, and only one-third of the rifles needed for its own army [190]. Ludendorff believed that the Americans contributed significantly to the final Allied offensive simply by taking over quiet sectors from veteran French and British units [9]. Yet the realization that the American army would become increasingly competent and strong in 1919 convinced the German High Command that it was futile to continue the war [63; 96]. 'Although there was little doubt in the minds of the soldiers of the AEF – from General Pershing to the lowliest doughboy – that the Americans had won the war on the western front, a more accurate assessment is that the Allies might have lost the war without the American Expeditionary Forces', concludes historian Allan Millett [110 *p. 251*].

THE AMERICAN SOLDIER EXPERIENCE

It is difficult to characterize a typical soldier experience. In the Civil War, 90 percent of all men who served were combatant troops. In the First World War, the experience of combat only accurately described the wartime ordeal of 40 percent of troops. Keeping the organization running and supplying front-line troops occupied the time of the other 60 percent. Deciding who is a typical American is another reason it is difficult to generalize about their wartime experience. Overall, 15 percent of all adult American men served in the war but immigrants, African-Americans, and Native Americans all served in numbers larger than their proportional representation in the population. Approximately 18 percent of the entire force (numbering half a million) were foreign-born. African-Americans made up 13 percent of the wartime forces though they were only 10 percent of the country's population, while at least 25 percent of the Native American male population served in the war. The army's different treatment of each group reflected the societal debates over what the future should hold for each group [118]. Progressive reformers, minority organizations, civilian communities near training camps, and soldiers themselves all influenced the army's treatment of immigrant, Native American and African-American soldiers.

The desire to assimilate immigrants influenced the army's handling of ethnic soldiers. Military training required all recruits to shed civilian habits and adopt military ones, but the army did not adopt 100 percent Americanism as its approach to dealing with immigrant soldiers. Instead, the army sought advice from moderate Progressive social reformers and developed a plan to segregate immigrant soldiers temporarily into ethnic units so they could learn English, receive military training, and also maintain cultural traditions [100]. Community leaders supported the plan to segregate ethnic soldiers to protect their dual identity as Polish-Americans or Italian-Americans. All agreed that the eventual goal was to prepare immigrant soldiers for assignment in regular army units. Many immigrant soldiers served in regular army combatant units, and while ethnic slurs were a common part of the soldiers' vocabulary, there were no widespread objections among native-born soldiers to serving with immigrants. At the end of their service, many of these troops became American citizens. The army's benign treatment of immigrant soldiers, however, did not quell concerns that America was being over-run by untrustworthy immigrants or prevent the country from adopting strict post-war limits on immigration.

The expectation of eventual assimilation was also the goal for Native American groups. Some Native American groups wanted segregated units to protect their way of life. The War Department refused, remembering the poor showing of experimental Indian units in the 1890s, and most philanthropic groups saw the war as an opportunity to hasten assimilation [117]. There was little incentive to segregate Indian soldiers since white soldiers were enthusiastic about serving with a group they considered a warrior race. The view that Indians were natural fighters was widespread. President Wilson was fond of repeating the apocryphal story of an Indian soldier who complained that the training camp regime contained 'too much salute, not enough shoot' [95 p. 277]. The army made no effort to help Native Americans protect their cultural traditions. A new generation with combat experience, however, gave many tribes the chance to resurrect warrior societies and mourning rituals which children born after the end of the Indian Wars had never seen. Native Americans benefited significantly from their participation in the war. Congress dropped its previous demand that Indians give up their tribal rights to become American citizens when it granted full citizenship rights in 1924 to thank Native Americans for their support of the war.

African-American troops served in all-black units mostly under white officers. This division reflected white Americans' widespread acceptance of segregation as a permanent solution to troublesome race relations [14; 23]. Most black advancement leaders grudgingly accepted segregated units and a segregated camp to train black officers. They put faith in the hope that the black community's loyalty during the war would prompt white America to recognize their rights as citizens [16; 20; 21]. In a controversial decision, the civil rights activist W. E. B. Du Bois urged African-Americans to close ranks with white Americans for the duration of the war [*Doc. 6*]. He was later criticized for this call for unity after it became clear that the war had aggravated, rather than improved, race relations in the United States. Black soldiers received few chances to demonstrate their bravery or their capacity to lead. Southern communities soon forced the army to abandon initial plans to train large numbers of black conscripts as combatants. After black regular army soldiers participated in a riot in Houston on 25 August 1917, Southern opposition to teaching more black men how to handle firearms solidified [19]. 'It is not so much that they fear that the Negro will strike if he gets a chance, but rather that they assume with curious unanimity that he has *reason* to strike, that any other person in his circumstances or treated as he is would rebel,' W. E. B. Du Bois later commented about the white South's fear of training black men to shoot rifles [15 *p. 602*]. It was not difficult for racist army officials to agree that 80 percent of black troops should serve in assorted labor battalions, pioneer infantry units, salvage companies, and stevedore organizations. Serving in these units disappointed many black soldiers, since they knew that few honors went to those who labored behind the lines. Nonetheless, these troops performed important logistical services without which a modern army could not stay in the field for any length of time.

The army only organized two black fighting Divisions, the 92nd and 93rd. Their different experiences revealed more about the inevitable effect of discrimination than the innate fighting abilities of black men. The 92nd Division was ill-fated from the beginning. The division never trained its troops together because its units were scattered among various northern training camps [14; 23]. The effects of poor training were apparent in a dismal initial showing during the Meuse–Argonne campaign. White officers later used the panicked performance of African-Americans as evidence of their cowardice. The other black combatant unit, the provisional 93rd Division, contained four infantry regiments which served with the French army. The French had no qualms about training black men to fight, having already raised a large colonial force from their African territories. Some French officials hoped that the amalgamation of black Americans into the French army would serve as the first step towards blending the two armies permanently. With proper training and confident leadership, these soldiers performed well and the French government decorated many in recognition of their valiant service at the front. The 93rd provided the black community with two genuine war heroes, Sergeant Henry Johnson and Private Needham Roberts, who fought valiantly when a German raiding party surprised them in an observation post. Despite being wounded, Johnson and Roberts killed four Germans and wounded thirty-two [14].

Southern white soldiers brought their prejudices into the army, and army officials struggled throughout the war to prevent tensions between white and black soldiers from escalating into outright rioting. The absence of segregated transportation and recreational facilities in France, combined with the vote of confidence given by the French to their fighting abilities made the distinction between France and the United States easy for African-Americans to make. The French army was well aware of the racial tensions which plagued the American army. During the war, one key French liaison official noted that 'the American point of view on the "Negro question" may appear questionable to the French mind, [but] American opinion is unanimous ... ' [104 *p. 26*]. In this analysis, Colonel Linard described how the amicable working relationships which French officers had established with American black officers and soldiers horrified American whites. Linard took care to note that American white soldiers were particularly 'outraged by all public intimacy between white women and blacks'. For the sake of preserving American goodwill, Linard recommended that French officers and civilians maintain a social distance from American blacks. This analysis was transmitted to each commandant in the French army, then abruptly canceled two days later. When Du Bois received a copy of this memo after the war, he commended France for refusing to institute Jim Crow practices. The letter from Sergeant Charles Isum [*Doc. 7*] discusses his own confrontations with white Americans in France. The warm welcome from French civilians that Isum describes caused many African-American soldiers to return home feeling that in France they finally understood how freedom felt. 'You know now that the mean, contemptible spirit of race prejudice that curses this land is not the spirit of other lands: you know now what it is to be treated as a man was like to be treated like real American men', the Reverend F. J. Grimké told a group of returned African-American soldiers in 1919 [1 *p. 242*].

The army's experience with minority soldiers demonstrates that the demands of the majority white population exerted enormous influence over manpower policies within the wartime army. Yet it was harder for white soldiers to control other aspects of their military career. Americans came into the war late, but they were not able to escape its horrors. Many American soldiers entered the war expecting a great adventure. As one soldier later recalled, they '...were simply fascinated by the prospect of adventure and heroism. ... Here was our one great chance for excitement and risk. We could not afford to pass it up' [106 *p. xviii*]. Indeed, the most memorable wartime experience for some soldiers who arrived too late to fight or soldiers who served behind the lines was the chance to tour France [75; 108]. Many others, however, even those who never left the training camps, found the war anything but a romantic, heroic interlude. The poverty and devastation of France, coupled with the reality of harsh, arbitrary military discipline, dashed the initial idealism of many who never got anywhere near the front. In addition, the Spanish influenza pandemic which ravaged American training camps in 1918 ensured that no one was guaranteed of surviving the war.

Disease was a traditional problem for wartime armies. The Army Medical Department aggressively inspected water supplies and sewage systems, the traditional conduits of contagious diseases. Despite this rigor, most stateside camps experienced short epidemics of measles or spinal meningitis that medical officers contained primarily through quarantines. In 1918, however, there was not much either civilian or military physicians could do to combat a vicious strain of influenza that struck the young adult male population, normally the least likely to succumb to respiratory infections, particularly hard [53]. Between 1 September 1918 and 11 November 1918 approximately 9,000 AEF soldiers and 23,000 stateside soldiers died from this mysterious virus. The virus struck without warning, within an hour or two victims had raging fevers and severe body aches. Many recovered from this phase of the illness, but 10 percent developed pneumonia and died a few days later after their lungs filled with fluid and suffocated them. During this period nearly the same number (35,000) of American soldiers died from influenza as had died from combat wounds [99]. The close confines of training camps apparently exposed many to the disease, though scientists are still uncertain how the disease was transmitted. Biologists speculate that in the spring of 1918 the influenza germ appeared as a mutated version of swine influenza in the American Mid-West. American soldiers carried the infection to France where it rapidly spread among the enlisted population in overseas training camps and throughout Europe, Africa, and Asia. Outbreaks were also reported in Central America. The pandemic acquired its name because the neutral Spanish press, unfettered by censorship regulations, reported the full extent of the epidemic, thus leading many to conclude that this was where the disease originated. In August, American sailors brought back to Boston the more deadly second strain of the disease from France. American infection rates from the first strain were relatively low, but the second wave devastated the American civilian population. Public officials closed movie houses and schools in an effort to contain the epidemic. Then suddenly, after the epidemic ran its course, the virus disappeared as mysteriously as it had come. Overall, the Spanish influenza pandemic had a catastrophic effect worldwide. From 1918–19, the disease killed 25 million people, including half a million Americans. By comparison, 7.5 million men died in battle between 1914 and 1918 [2]. The bloodiest war ever known thus coincided with the deadliest influenza virus yet recorded.

Front-line troops were not immune to Spanish influenza, but for some reason rear-area soldiers bore the brunt of the epidemic. Only front-line soldiers, however, suffered the mental breakdowns that became known as shell-shock. All battle accounts include some mention of soldiers collapsing from the strain of continuous artillery bombardments, the sight of bodies blown to bits, wearing tight gas masks for hours, or sheer exhaustion. Men diagnosed with shell-shock suffered from nightmares, panic attacks, and some could not sleep or speak. Private Duncan Kemerer, a member of the 111th Infantry, 28th Division, arrived at the base hospital in such poor condition that the sound of a spoon dropping sent him frantically searching for cover under his bed. After resting and eating well for a few days, however, Kemerer returned to his unit [82]. Field psychiatrists considered this a rational and sane decision to make. If rest and food were not enough to convince men to take this step once the tremors had stopped and speech and memory returned, field psychiatrists emphasized to each man that their comrades needed them and that the glory of victory would be lost to them forever if they failed to return to the front. Men usually responded to these appeals to their honor, masculinity, duty, and ambition. Whether these soldiers were cured is another question [114]. Three out of every five beds in government hospitals were filled in the inter-war period with veterans suffering from shell-shock. Anecdotal evidence also underscores that many veterans had difficulty forgetting the wartime horrors they had witnessed. Three years after returning home, for instance, Walter Zukowski was not alone in noting that he was still fighting the war in his dreams [82]. Many other veterans described themselves as nervous, jumpy, and unstable for years afterwards.

INTERVENTION IN NORTH RUSSIA AND SIBERIA

The experiences of American troops who fought in Russia during the war differed dramatically from those of soldiers in France. The American military intervention in Siberia and North Russia was an extraordinary escapade which kept some American soldiers fighting until 1920 [Map 1]. In 1918, twenty different governments claimed power on Russian soil, therefore the eventual outcome of the Russian revolution was very much in doubt. As Russia collapsed into civil war, the Wilson administration began aiding anti-bolshevik movements by sending covert financial aid through Allied governments, smuggling in military supplies, conducting sabotage missions, and organizing an extensive intelligence-gathering operation [26]. Wilson at first opposed direct intervention for both pragmatic and principled reasons. The President worried that armed intervention might backfire and help the weak bolshevik government rally together Russians who opposed the presence of foreign armies on their soil. He also was wary of undermining his own call in the Fourteen Points for the world to give Russia 'an unhampered and unembarrassed opportunity for the independent determination of her own political development and national policy...' [*Doc. 3*]. The British took a different stand. They pushed for an immediate military response to prevent Germany from seizing stockpiled Allied supplies and transferring troops to the western front.

Knowing that the Allies were angry that the United States refused to amalgamate the American and Allied armies, Wilson finally decided to make a gesture of goodwill and give in to British demands [31; 36]. Secretary of War Baker later recalled that 'the only real disagreement I ever had with President Wilson was about the sending of American troops to North Russia. ... The expedition was nonsense from the beginning' [31 *p. 442*, n. 54]. Chief of Staff Peyton March shared his view, Baker noted, but Wilson countered that while the two were no doubt right 'from a military point of view ... my trouble is that we are fighting the war with allies' who had 'so much set their hearts' on intervention [36 *p. 443*]. The changing fortunes of the Czech Legion played a role in Wilson's decision as well [29]. Stranded along the eastern front when Russia abruptly ended its war with Germany, the Czechs called on the Allies to come and help them reach the western front. The plight of these popular fighters battling their way out of the interior of Russia captured the imagination of the Americans. Wilson also agreed to intervene once he found a way to reconcile the mission with his principle of self-determination. He now argued that the American presence would give the Russian people the military protection they needed to express their true desire for democracy [26].

The July 1918 decision to intervene in Siberia was influenced by these, as well as other factors. In the view of some historians, Wilson's hatred of Bolshevism was so strong that it alone accounted for his decision to intervene in Siberia [27; 32; 38]. Wilson did not authorize the Siberian mission until the Czechs had established control over most of the Trans-Siberian Railway and appeared to be rallying a significant number of anti-bolshevik Russians to their side [26]. Instead of leaving Russia, the Czechs agreed to serve as the fighting nucleus of the Allied forces. A further enticement for Wilson to join the expedition was the unwelcome Japanese offer, which the Supreme War Council accepted in February 1918, to intervene in Siberia on behalf of the Allies. Thwarting Japan's imperialistic ambitions in Siberia, some historians argue, was more important to Wilson than crushing Bolshevism with force [26; 37].

American troops had two quite different experiences in North Russia and Siberia. In Siberia, 8,388 regular army troops came directly from the Philippines to join an Allied expedition that included Japanese, British, French, Chinese, Canadian, and Italian troops. Their main task was to guard the Trans-Siberian Railway in order to keep supply lines open for the Czechs and to free White Russian troops for combat against the Red Army. Major General William S. Graves, the expedition commander, struggled to stay neutral as counter-revolutionary groups vied for control of Siberia but the

Americans were unable to avoid a few deadly clashes with rival White factions. In June 1919, Wilson finally chose to back strongman Admiral Aleksandr V. Kolchak and directed American financial and military aid to Kolchak until his government fell in November [26]. With military odds dwindling and increased opposition at home, the Americans began withdrawing in January 1920. They left the Czechs to fight and bargain their own way out of Siberia by turning Kolchak over to the Bolsheviks.

Five thousand miles away in North Russia, 5,710 drafted troops serving in the 339th Infantry Regiment, one battalion from the 310th Engineers, 337th Field Hospital and 337th Ambulance Company of the 85th Division joined 11,130 British, French and locally recruited Russian soldiers to complete the Allied detachment. In his *aide-mémoire* authorizing the mission Wilson provided both limited and open-ended goals for American troops in North Russia. In one sentence, Wilson restricted American activities to guarding the port city of Archangel to provide a way for Czech troops to escape. But in another, he vaguely offered American assistance 'to steady any efforts at self-government or self-defense in which the Russians themselves may be willing to accept assistance' [31 *p. 56*]. British commanders of the mission seized on this ambiguous phrase to fit their broader goals. Instead of limited guard duty, American soldiers found themselves actively pursuing and fighting Bolshevik forces along a so-called defensive front which extended over 300 miles.

Wilson accused the British of misrepresenting the extent of Russian support in order to use American troops to further their goal of re-opening the eastern front. The President lost faith in the North Russian expedition and refused requests for further deployments. It soon appeared that his worst fears were coming true. Too small to inspire anti-Bolsheviks or indifferent peasants to run the risk of supporting the counter-revolution, the North Russian expedition helped the Bolsheviks save their faltering regime by galvanizing the Russian people to oppose the foreign invasion. Bolshevik propaganda successfully caste domestic opponents as collaborators with the invading powers, and easy victories against the out-manned Allies made the Bolsheviks appear stronger than they were in 1919 and further discouraged dissidents from organizing armed opposition [26].

Wilson did not, however, authorize the withdrawal of the American contingent before ice blocked the port in November, thus guaranteeing that American soldiers would fight in North Russia until the spring. Despite mounting opposition in Congress, advice to withdraw from his military commanders, and his own conclusion that the expedition was a failure, Wilson refused to authorize the withdrawal until he spoke with Allied leaders at the peace conference. When Wilson's attempt to negotiate a diplomatic closure to the Allied intervention failed, the President finally agreed to withdraw American troops when the ice broke in the spring.

The planned June evacuation was announced in February, but this information only haphazardly reached troops or was discounted as a rumor by others. Allied troops were in a tenuous strategic position that winter as supply lines broke down and enemy forces grew. In mid-January a rout by the revitalized Sixth Soviet Army at Shenkursk forced American troops to retreat fifty miles to the rear before they could stabilize the front. Outnumbered, forced to slog through miles of frozen terrain to confront an enemy they could barely identify, and unsure of their mission, it was no surprise that troop discontent was soon evident. Scribbled notations in private diaries, intercepted messages from those trying to send the truth home, self-inflicted wounds, and timid responses to bolshevik overtures of friendship revealed near-mutinous conditions in the ranks. In secretly-circulated petitions and direct confrontations with their officers, troops demanded to know why they were required to continue fighting months after the war with Germany had ended. In one petition, First Lieutenant Carl H. Christine declared, 'we have earnestly endeavored to find some justification for our being here, but we have been unable to reconcile this expedition with American ideals and principles instilled within us' [*Doc. 8*]. In March 1919 word arrived in the United States that a company of men had refused to load their sleds and return to the front. The March mutiny became a *cause célèbre* at home even though the men had returned to the front after their commanding officer agreed to listen to their questions [34]. American forces left North Russia when the ports re-opened in June, seven months after the Armistice. During a stop-over in France, several soldiers came down the gangplank and asked sarcastically if the war was over.

The North Russian Expedition offers a particularly good example of how politicians, generals, and enlisted troops experienced the same event differently and how compromises with the Allies affected how, when, and where American troops fought. Within the rest of the American army, there were also important differences between how combatants and non-combatants, blacks and whites, foreign and native-born soldiers experienced the war. The quality of leadership, overall strategy pursued, compromises with the Allies, and American troops' relationships with one another all affected how the American army fought and won the war.

CHAPTER FIVE

PEACE

On the 11th hour of the 11th day of the 11th month of 1918 the Armistice went into effect and guns fell silent along the western front. 'I've lived through the war!,' exclaimed an American airman, but statisticians counted nine million soldiers who were not so lucky [55 p. 501]. War conditions killed another five million civilians worldwide, including 750,000 German civilians who were dead because of the Allied blockade. The casuality list reached 38 million if the wounded or missing were included.

The end did not come easily for Germany. One by one Germany's allies left the war. The Ottoman Empire capitulated on 30 October 1918, followed by the Austro-Hungarian Empire on 4 November. Meanwhile, the German imperial government was crumbling, partly due to the parliamentary reforms that Wilson demanded as a pre-condition for peace negotiations, partly because it was becoming clearer and clearer that Germany had lost the war. The political crisis worsened when a mutiny in the German navy triggered widespread strikes in German cities. On 9 November, Kaiser Wilhelm II abdicated. When revolutionaries temporarily seized the imperial palace and proclaimed Germany a soviet republic, the Kaiser fled to Holland. Two days later, the Armistice came into effect.

The war was over, but the challenge of formulating a just peace was just beginning. The desire for revenge against Germany was strong, even though the international community knew it needed to go beyond punishing Germany and craft a settlement that established permanent peace in Europe. When the peace negotiations were completed, the United States faced a critical decision about its role in the world. Had its participation in the war and its advocacy of democracy made it a world power, responsible for more than the welfare of its own people? Peace also involved more than settling world problems. For soldiers, it meant that they would soon return home. Would the government help them make the difficult re-adjustment to their old civilian lives? This chapter will discuss these issues, and evaluate what lessons Americans drew from the war. The world, the nation, and individuals were about to realize that the war was a crucial event which had changed American society forever.

THE PARIS PEACE SETTLEMENT

'The simple man on the street cannot understand what has happened', noted one German civilian when the Armistice was announced [55 *p. 507*]. Why had the German army surrendered while it was still on foreign soil? Pershing also believed the Armistice was premature. 'What I dread is that Germany doesn't know that she was licked,' he noted soon afterwards, 'Had they given us another week, we'd have taught them' [190 *p. 232*]. German nationalists and Nazis later blamed defeat on a 'stab in the back' at home, and repeatedly pointed out that Allied armies never pierced the German border until they entered as a post-war occupying force. The political and social turmoil in Germany, however, was a reflection rather than the cause of Germany's defeat. There was no question that by November Germany had lost the war on land and at sea. The Allies had captured one-fourth of the German army and half of its guns. Meanwhile, the Allied blockade and convoy* system was denying Germany the imports it needed to continue the war and feed its people [63]. In 1918, the Allies started using convoys in which merchant ships were grouped together under the protection of battleships. This system effectively ensured an uninterrupted flow of supplies to Britain and France [Map 2]. The declaration of unconditional submarine warfare had brought the United States into the war, but now German U-boats could not reach their targets without exposing themselves to the new depth charges and sonars carried by battleships. German submarine captains were just learning to coordinate attacks on small convoys and make surface night attacks when the war ended. They would perfect these tactics in the Second World War.

In many other respects, the Second World War would pick up where the First World War left off. Every step of the peace process seemed to be setting the stage for the future. In the Forest of Compiègne behind the French lines, representatives from both sides met to set the terms for the armistice. This spot became a French national monument after the war, the place where the Germans agreed, among other things, to withdraw from France, surrender its submarine fleet, and accept the presence of an Allied occupying force. It was no accident that Adolph Hitler returned to Compiègne in 1940 to receive the French surrender on the same spot where Germany had accepted these humiliating terms in 1918. The Germans took the boxcar back to Berlin where it attracted thousands of tourists during the war. They finally destroyed it in 1945 as Allied armies neared the city to prevent yet another surrender from occurring in it.

The Armistice ended active fighting, but the details of the peace settlement took months to negotiate. Twenty-seven nations and four British Dominions sent delegates and huge staffs of experts to the Paris Peace Conference. The critical discussions took place between Wilson, Clemenceau, the British Prime Minister Lloyd George, and the Italian Premier Vittorio

Orlando in the Council of Four. This group for a short time was the Council of Three when Orlando left briefly to protest at the denial of Italian territorial demands [148].

In the end, few were satisfied with the peace settlement. In 1917, Wilson had noted that 'only a peace between equals can last', but Germany was excluded from the negotiations [162 *p. 323*]. Instead, the Allies presented Germany with a completed treaty to sign. Foch read the terms of the Versailles Peace Treaty* and exclaimed, 'this isn't a peace, it's a twenty year truce' [58 *p. 1151*]. The continuation of the British blockade and melting away of their army gave Germany no choice except to sign the treaty under protest on 28 June 1919.

Key flaws in the Paris Peace Settlement (which included separate treaties with each Central Power) were the following:

1. The Versailles Peace Treaty required that Germany accept responsibility and pay for Allied civilian losses and damages caused 'as a consequence of the war imposed upon them by the aggression of Germany' [143 *p. 231*]. This famous 'war guilt' clause fueled the German desire for revenge against the Allies. There were historical precedents for reparations (France to Germany in 1871, more recently Russia to Germany), but these payments were nonetheless contentious. The Reparations Committee set Germany's bill at $33 billion in gold, but the amount owed was continuously scaled downwards in the 1920s. Whether the real reason was a German inability or unwillingness to pay this debt, reparations were a constant source of post-war conflict between Germany and France [138; 149].

2. The dismemberment of the Russian, German and Austro-Hungarian empires created new political problems in Europe [Map 4]. Wilson's principle of self-determination was reflected in the re-drawn map of eastern Europe which fulfilled the nationalistic ambitions of ethnic groups in Czechoslovakia, Poland, Yugoslavia, Croatia, Latvia, Lithuania, and Estonia. The desires of German-speaking peoples in Poland, Czechoslovakia, and Austria to unite with Germany, however, were disregarded. Lloyd George warned against strewing 'Europe with Alsace-Lorraines', an allusion to how Germany's annexation of these French provinces in 1871 made reconciliation between the two countries impossible afterwards [55 *p. 513*]. Without western support, these independent states were weak and vulnerable to German and Soviet expansionist schemes. Hitler justified his invasions of Czechoslovakia (1938), then Poland (1939) as a drive to reunite the German-speaking world. The *cordon sanitaire* of independent states created out of the territories Russia lost to Germany in 1918 was intended to protect the west from Bolshevism. The Bolsheviks failed to reconquer this territory

in the early 1920s, but the Soviet Union successfully recovered much of it during the Second World War.

3. At the peace conference, a twenty-five-year-old Vietnamese named Nguyen Ai Quoc submitted a petition to Wilson seeking equal rights before the law and an end to forced labor in the French colony. Wilson refused to receive it and Nguyen Ai Quoc (who later changed his name to Ho Chi Minh) found a better reception for his ideas in the new Soviet Union. Self-determination was a principle reserved for eastern Europe. In the Middle East, Africa, and Asia, the peace conference essentially transferred colonial possessions from the losers (the Ottoman and German empires) to the victors. In theory, the new mandate* system named a western nation as a League of Nations trustee for territories in need of instruction before they assumed the responsibilities of self-government. In reality, the mandate system simply cloaked old-style imperialism in the new, modern rhetoric of self-determination. Any hopes that the war would end imperialism were over. The ideals Wilson stated in the Fourteen Points, however, fueled emerging anti-colonial movements and set the stage for future wars of independence. The rejection of Nguyen Ai Quoc's petition, and other seemingly insignificant events at the conference, such as the competing claims of Zionists and Arab nationalists in the new British mandate of Palestine, foreshadowed crucial world crises to come.

4. The Treaty established a League of Nations, but there were critical questions about how collective security would ensure a peaceful future. Were countries agreeing to give up control of their armies and the power to declare war to the League? Senator Henry Cabot Lodge, the principal American opponent of the Versailles Treaty, acknowledged that he was as moved by tributes to eternal peace as the next man. But, he asked the American people, 'are you ready to put your soldiers and your sailors at the disposition of other nations?' [153 *p. 49*]. The US Senate never ratified the Versailles Treaty and the United States never joined the League of Nations. Without American membership, there was no hope of the organization serving as more than a place to air grievances.

5. Finally, the treaty's provisions divided the Allies in the post-war world. Uneasy about the harsh terms, Britain became sympathetic to German complaints and developed a policy of appeasement towards Germany in the 1930s that ended in disaster. The guarantee of American military support for French borders evaporated after the United States rejected the treaty. France consequently reacted violently to any sign of German resurgence and sought alliances with the states on Germany's eastern border. Italy harbored resentments over territories denied to them, a humiliation which the fascist leader Benito Mussolini vowed to avenge when he seized power in 1922. Japan was stung at the treaty's failure to

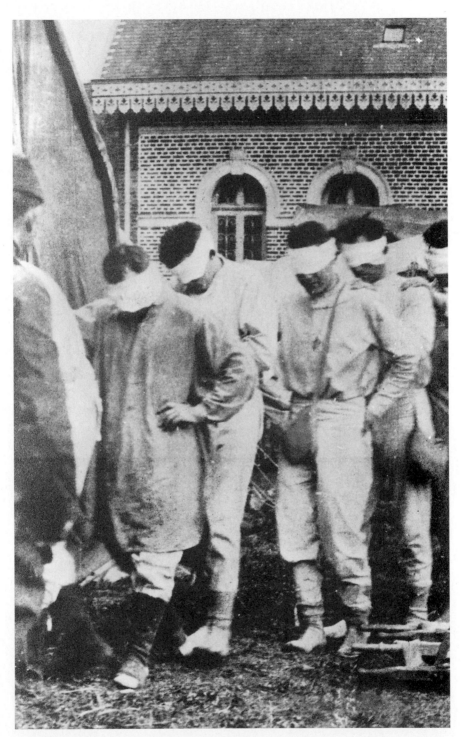

1. American soldiers who temporarily lost their eyesight in France as a consequence of poison gas attacks.

2. U.S. Army soldiers manoeuvre machine gun through blasted wood and thick fog, 1918.

3. Illustrating how unprepared the American Army was in 1917 to fight in the trench warfare conditions along the Western Front, this photo shows American soldiers training in the United States for the type of massed, flag-waving charges across the open battlefield used in the Civil and Spanish-American Wars.

4. General John J. Pershing emphasized the importance of hand-to-hand combat in his training doctrine, and here American soldiers practice using their bayonets to capture an enemy trench.

5. American soldiers get a firsthand view of the war's devastation.

6. Total war required the active participation of all Americans, including these women and children who are posting propaganda posters urging men to enlist.

7. American soldier prepared for a gas attack.

8. The Avenue des Allies, New York City. For the duration of the Fourth Liberty Loan, Fifth Avenue is called the Avenue des Allies. It is decorated with the flags of the twenty-two nations now at war with Germany.

incorporate a statement protecting the rights of non-white nations into the League Covenant [140]. Japan's refusal to be considered a second-rate 'yellow' people fed the expansionist drive that would eventually pit the Japanese against their former Allies.

Why was the peace so flawed? The most popular figure in the world on Armistice Day was Woodrow Wilson. The news that Wilson was taking the unprecedented step for an American President and making the long journey to France to negotiate the treaty himself raised even higher expectations [184]. As Wilson toured Paris, London, Rome, and Milan, papers greeted him as 'The Moses from Across the Atlantic' and 'The Savior of Humanity' [139 *p. 195*]. Wilson was determined to create a lasting world peace. European leaders, however, knew that their compatriots' desire for revenge was strong, despite the crowds gathering to see the American President. At first glance, it appeared that America's strong army, ample food supplies, and ready cash gave Wilson all the cards that he needed to force the exhausted Europeans to comply with his demands [138]. But Wilson had domestic political problems which weakened his position. In November, the Republicans had seized control of Congress. Wilson had asked the country to return a Democratic majority to Congress in the mid-term election of 1918 as a vote of confidence for his Fourteen Points peace proposal. The reasons for this mid-term Democratic loss were complex, and Wilson was correct in believing that many in the country still supported his peace proposals. Still, Wilson severely underestimated conservative resistance to his version of progressive internationalism and the determination of Lodge, the Republican chairman of the Senate Foreign Relations Committee.

Losing control of his legislature weakened Wilson's stature in the eyes of Clemenceau and Lloyd George, who had just won overwhelming votes of confidence in their own legislative elections with the campaign promise to make Germany pay. Clemenceau and Lloyd George knew how to use Wilson's political difficulties to their advantage because they understood that his bottom line was to secure a League of Nations at practically any cost. One by one, Wilson compromised his principles of peace without victory, freedom of the seas, and self-determination to attain this goal [188]. Much of the Versailles Treaty reflects the French desire to protect its borders with a demilitarized zone, its future by forcing Germany disarmament, and its economy by assuming ownership of German mines in the Saar region to compensate for the ones a retreating German army destroyed in the north of France. In addition, the French pushed for high reparations and mutual defense pacts with the United States and Britain. Wilson was often accused of being too idealistic, but was it realistic to argue for money Germany could or would not pay, an admission of guilt they did not feel, and base hopes for future security on Allied armies that would not come [142]?

Clemenceau, however, was in a good position to achieve his goals. Unlike Wilson, he was not trying to reform the world; he was only interested in protecting France. Accordingly, he chaired meetings by taking naps when the issues did not concern him. Wilson, on the other hand, was worn down by the constant haggling on every issue and soon was willing to make compromises so he could leave and attend to his political problems at home.

After completing much of the actual treaty, including the League of Nations Covenant, Wilson returned briefly to the United States in mid-February. Attacks from Republicans that Wilson had ignored American national interests convinced the President that the treaty as written would face an uncertain future in the Senate. Consequently, when Wilson returned to France on 13 March 1919, he requested concessions to appease his political opponents. The new American demands included international recognition of the Monroe Doctrine and the ability for countries to withdraw from the League, placed immigration and tariffs out of the League's control, and gave America the right to refuse territorial mandates from the League. Wilson also returned to the conference determined to guarantee American acceptance of the League by incorporating the League so firmly into the text of the peace treaty that the Senate could not reject the League without also rejecting the treaty, a step he never imagined the Senate would take. With the American President beginning the second phase of negotiations with a list of demands from his countrymen, there was little reason for other members of the Council of Four to exercise restraint in pressing for concessions to satisfy their home populations [60]. Wilson was well aware of the flaws in the final treaty which he accurately predicted would bring another war in twenty years [188]. But he hoped that the passage of time and the League of Nations would ameliorate its worst excesses.

When Wilson returned home with the completed treaty, the outpouring of public support for the League of Nations was impressive. A majority of state legislatures, governors, and newspapers advocated American membership. Yet neither the treaty nor the decision for ratification was decided by referendum. Instead, the fate of the treaty was now in the hands of the Senate. Republican opposition increasingly focused on Article 10 of the League Covenant. Consider the wording of the article and the concerns it was bound to raise. Article 10 read:

> The Members of the League undertake to respect and preserve as against external aggression the territorial integrity and existing political independence of all the members of the League. In case of any such aggression or in case of any threat or danger of such aggression the Council shall advise upon the means by which this obligation shall be fulfilled. [13 *p. 14*]

Lodge maintained that this clause overrode the constitutional right of Congress to declare war or authorize the use of US military forces. His main objections are reprinted in Document 9. Lodge proposed adding a reservation to the treaty which explicitly said that 'the United States assumes no obligation to preserve the territorial integrity or political independence of any other country or to interfere in controversies between nations' unless Congress gave explicit approval [7 *p. 211*]. Lodge was skeptical of collective security; instead he believed that a new balance of power structure was the best way to assure peace. Overall, Lodge proposed fourteen reservations he wanted to add to the treaty. Wilson refused to accept them because, he argued, adding American reservations to the treaty would require renegotiation with all its signatories. Whether Wilson was right on this point is open to debate. When the Chinese tried to accept the treaty but reject the provision which gave Japan control over Shantung, the Council of Four had agreed with Clemenceau that 'a Treaty which was signed with reservations was not a treaty' [182 *p. 192*]. As the treaty fight in the Senate unfolded, however, voices from the other side of the Atlantic argued that it would be in Europe's interest to accept whatever reservations were needed to ensure that America played an active role in maintaining peace in the post-war world [184]. It was quite possible, then, that Europe would have grumbled but then accepted the American conditions. From the standpoint of American jurisprudence, renegotiation was required only if the Senate added amendments, not reservations, to the treaty.

Since Wilson had compromised with the Allies, it was entirely possible that Wilson intended to use this unyielding position as a negotiating strategy. Once the Senate vote was imminent, and Wilson could be sure that Lodge would not come up with other reservations to thwart ratification, perhaps he intended to bend [137]. For the moment, however, Wilson stood firm.

Turning directly to the public, Wilson undertook a huge speaking tour to defend the treaty. In three weeks he traveled 10,000 miles and made forty speeches to hundreds of thousands of people [139]. He tried to dismiss concerns about Article 10 as impractical, assuring an audience in Salt Lake City, Utah,

> If you want to put out a fire in Utah, you don't send to Oklahoma for the fire engine. If you want to put out a fire in the Balkans, if you want to stamp out the smoldering flames in some part of Central Europe, you don't send to the United States for troops. The Council of the League selects the powers which are most ready, most available, most suitable, and selects them at their own consent, so the United States would in no such circumstances conceivable be drawn in unless the flames spread to the world [8, vol. 63 *p. 453*].

These assurances, however, did not clarify exactly what America's moral and legal commitment to other countries would be if it agreed to 'respect and preserve' the territorial integrity and political independence of League members. Wilson was unwilling to acknowledge that this commitment represented a dramatic break with the traditional American foreign policy of avoiding entangling alliances. Instead, Wilson used his extraordinary oratory skills to bring an audience in Pueblo, Colorado to tears. 'Again and again, my fellow citizens, mothers who lost their sons in France have come to me and, taking my hand, have shed tears upon it ... ,' Wilson told the crowd, 'why should they weep upon my hand and call down the blessings of God upon me? Because they believe that their boys died for something that vastly transcends any of the immediate and palpable objectives of the war. They believe and rightly believe that their sons saved the liberty of the world' [8, vol. 63 *p. 511*]. Other excerpts from this speech are reprinted in Document 10.

This was the last speech the American people ever heard Wilson give in support of the treaty. Within hours of delivering these words, his doctor rushed a twitching and nauseated Wilson back to Washington where two days later he suffered a stroke. His life in the balance and permanently paralyzed on his left side, Wilson spent the rest of his presidency hidden in the White House. Wilson, Lloyd George said, was 'as much a victim of the war as any soldier who died in the trenches' [75 *p. 361*].

Instead of using his collapse to win sympathetic support from Americans for his exertions in the name of world peace, the seriousness of his illness was kept secret. The President's secretary issued a statement attributing his collapse to exhaustion and assured the public that the President was resting comfortably. For weeks, however, Wilson only spent three hours a day out of bed and saw no one except his wife and physician [184]. Wilson was incapacitated but rejected all private suggestions that he resign, and still refused to accept any reservations to the treaty. Whether this stubbornness was due to his personality, his convictions, or symptomatic of a stroke-induced mental impairment still provokes heated disagreement among historians [192]. Regardless of the real reason, Wilson's refusal to tell his party to compromise doomed the treaty to defeat.

On 19 November 1919, the Senate rejected the original treaty and the treaty with Lodge's reservations. The treaty with reservations failed once again to secure the two-thirds vote needed for ratification on 19 March 1920. Instead, on 2 July 1921, Congress approved a resolution officially ending the war with Germany. In October, the Senate ratified separate peace treaties with Germany, Austria, and Hungary.

Were Wilson's failures great enough to consider him the architect of the Second World War? Does comparing the Treaty of Brest-Litovsk with the Versailles Peace Treaty reveal that the ideals stated in the Fourteen Points were no match for the passions the war unleashed? Did the peace need to be just in order to last? These are difficult, but important questions students should consider when evaluating the peace treaties.

The peace settlement was destined to shape the course of world history. Wilson's hand in the peace meant that his legacy would endure as well. As historian Page Smith notes, Wilson was a flawed man. He was rigid, unyielding, preachy, supported racial segregation at home, and vindictive to his enemies. Yet, Smith continues,

> ... certain facts remain indisputable: He was a 'great man' in any proper meaning of those sometimes loosely used words; he changed the course of history; he expressed the highest ideals of America, ideals that have often been more honored in the breach than the observance, and did so with an eloquence that thrilled the souls of uncounted millions, not simply in the United States but all over the world. Almost single-handedly he created a global consciousness that looked beyond national divisions and ancient rivalries to a better human order and, finally, to peace. ... In aiming so high (and falling so far), he nonetheless opened a new chapter in the long history of the race, and those who walked in the light of his vision were not so as before. [59 *p. 828*]

Wilsonian ideals continue to inspire believers in democracy and peace worldwide.

THE LOST GENERATION, THE BONUS MARCH AND THE GI BILL

The war's outcome particularly disappointed the men who fought it. In the 1920s and 1930s, a celebrated generation of writers conveyed the anger and frustration of this 'lost generation' [75; 87]. Their novels were scathing indictments of bureaucratic bumbling, mindless patriotism, the brutality of combat, and lying propaganda. In *Company K*, William March assembled a series of 113 vignettes to portray how differently individual soldiers experienced the war's degradation. Among his fictionalized characters, Private Carroll Hart shoots down a German officer as he reaches inside his jacket. The man falls to the ground holding, not the expected grenade, but the photograph of a young girl. In the dark, Private Wilbur Bowden soothingly wraps his friend's legs, which he assumes are wounded, but Bowden's relief turns to horror when he realizes his friend has bled to death from a serious side wound he never noticed. In an ironic twist of fate, a character called 'The Unknown Soldier' dies on the barbed wire in No Man's Land after throwing away his identification tags to beat 'the orators and the wreath layers at their own game'. On 11 November 1921, the country buried an Unknown Soldier in Arlington Cemetery, Washington, DC. The day before the burial, 90,000 people paid their respects before the casket as it lay in the Rotunda of the Capitol surrounded by hundreds of wreaths [92]. This ceremony was the ultimate betrayal of March's 'unknown soldier' who died believing 'nobody will ever use me as a symbol. Nobody will ever tell lies over my dead body now!' [43 *p. 181*]. Another *Company K* character,

Private Harold Dresser, experiences a different sort of disillusionment. In his hometown, he notes, ' ... people point me out to strangers and say, "You'd never believe that fellow had a hat full of medals, would you?" And the strangers always say no, they never would' [43 *p. 225*]. Private Sylvester Wendell rebels against the task of writing soothing letters to the families of soldiers who will never return home.

> I gave every man a glorious, romantic death with appropriate last words, but after about the thirtieth letter, the lies I was telling began to gag me. I decided I'd tell the truth in at least one of the letters, and this is what I wrote: 'Dear Madam:
>
>> Your son, Francis, died needlessly in Belleau Wood. You will be interested to hear that at the time of his death he was crawling with vermin and weak from diarrhea. His feet were swollen and rotten and they stank. He lived like a frightened animal, cold and hungry. Then, on June 6th, a piece of shrapnel hit him and he died in agony, slowly. You'd never believe that he could live three hours, but he did. He lived three full hours screaming and cursing by turns. He had nothing to hold on to, you see: He had learned long ago that what he had been taught to believe by you, his mother, who loved him, under the meaningless names of honor, courage and patriotism, were all lies ... '. [43 *p. 101-2*]

Even in a fictional story, however, this mother never heard the truth about the war because Wendell tore the letter up after reading it to a friend. In his work, the acclaimed writer John Dos Passos described war as a machine that consumed the human soul. The excerpt from his masterpiece, *Three Soldiers*, reprinted in Document 11, protests the dehumanizing aspects of modern, industrialized warfare.

By 1921, most veterans were convinced the war had permanently changed their lives, even if they were not suffering directly from mental or physical injuries. Unable to find jobs in the post-war recession, veterans believed they had missed their chance to get ahead in life. During the war, workers received the highest wages in American history, while soldiers collected $30 a month. Even worse, wartime contracts guaranteed industrialists generous profits. Veterans believed the federal government had failed to balance the financial burden of the war equally between civilians and soldiers. To rectify this past injustice, they agitated for adjusted compensation. In 1924, veterans settled for a bond certificate that matured in 1945, rather than an immediate cash settlement [91]. With the economy improving, veterans accepted this compromise, satisfied the country had acknowledged its monetary debt to them.

Five years later, however, the Great Depression caused veterans to change their minds about waiting for their bonus money. Suddenly, this generation faced the prospect of starting over, not just once, but twice in their lives. Stories relating the imminent loss of a home, the catastrophe of successive crop failures, the inability to clothe children, and the shame of finally going on relief were common after the stock market crash of 1929. But veterans' stories of hardship started when they came back in 1919 to find 'foreigners' in factory jobs, women in clerical positions, and the chance to learn a skill gone. They worked hard and struggled to accumulate a small house and garden. They then told of losing a job, home, farm, or family after 1929.

On 29 May 1932, a small contingent of veterans from Portland, Oregon rode into the nation's capital atop eighteen trucks provided by the Maryland National Guard to present their demands for immediate payment personally to President Herbert Hoover. Heavy press coverage turned their odyssey into a fully-fledged mass movement. Over the next two months, 40,000 veterans participated in the Bonus March*. Many government officials viewed the Bonus Expeditionary Force (BEF) as a communist-inspired plot to overthrow the government. Veterans vigorously denied this charge. They set up a huge encampment called Camp Marks on the Anacostia Flats and proclaimed themselves a 'poor man's lobby'. The BEF resolved to stay in Washington until each veteran received his $1,500 bonus payment. When a measure to pay the bonus passed the House in June, the city waited apprehensively for the Senate to make its decision. Though defeat of the bill was certain, thousands of veterans amassed on the Capitol steps to hear the final verdict. At the White House, Hoover and his advisors worried that the Senators might grow fearful of the huge crowd outside and leave it to the President to veto the bill. Just in case the bill did pass, 300 armed guards waited in reserve with instructions to close and guard the gates of the White House [85; 86; 88].

To pass the time, the veterans whipped through a litany of their old war songs. The impromptu sing-along, so favored by camp welfare workers in 1918 as a way to keep morale high, included a parody of the AEF's signature song 'Over There'. The rousing words they had sung as soldiers were: 'Over There / Over There / Send the Word / Send the Word / Over There / That the Yanks are coming / The Yanks are coming / The drums rum-tuming everywhere'. Fourteen years later, veterans sang 'All you here / here and there / Pay the bonus, pay the bonus everywhere / For the Yanks are starving / the Yanks are starving everywhere' [11].

At 8:20 p.m., the Senate defeated the measure by a vote of 62–18. 'Prepare yourselves for a disappointment men,' BEF commander Walter Waters announced to a silent crowd [88 *p. 121*]. 'We are not telling you to go home. Go back to the camps!,' Waters shouted above the murmuring crowd [11]. After singing a hearty rendition of 'America', groups of men began trickling towards Camp Marks. The evening passed without incident.

Congress had voted, and Hoover now expected the marchers to pack up and leave. The BEF, however, showed no signs of dissipating naturally. New arrivals soon replaced marchers who left. Taking matters into their own hands, federal officials ordered the local police to take a small, first step and evict veterans from a set of downtown buildings that were due for demo-lition. During the eviction on 28 July 1932, a scuffle broke out between police and veterans, leaving two veterans dead. Fearing a riot, local officials called Hoover and asked for help from the army. Chief of Staff Douglas MacArthur, who had been anticipating trouble for some time, quickly mobilized nearby regular army troops. Despite receiving orders from Hoover to clear only the downtown camps, MacArthur decided to cross the Anacostia River and attack Camp Marks [89; 94]. In his midnight press con-ference, MacArthur expressed no second thoughts or reservations about using regular army troops to drive the veterans from the city or for burning their encampment. Instead, MacArthur proudly declared he had liberated the besieged people of Washington from the grip of a force whose terrorizing presence recalled the brutal German occupation of northern France during the war [102]. This time MacArthur escaped unscathed for his insubordina-tion, but eventually his military career would end when he disobeyed President Harry Truman during the Korean War in 1951.

When presidential candidate Franklin D. Roosevelt (FDR) heard of the eviction he reportedly told an advisor 'Well, Felix, this will elect me' [89 *p. 285*]. As FDR predicted, the image of an uncaring Hoover who locked himself in the White House and sent troops to drive away starving men con-tributed to his re-election defeat in 1932.

Roosevelt, however, also opposed paying the bonus. Catering to special interest groups, he argued, would not end the Depression. This logic lost its appeal once the New Deal established programs specifically for farmers, businessmen, and the aged. Consequently, in 1936, Congress overrode a presidential veto and paid veterans their bonus.

After the next war, the First World War veterans were determined to give their sons a better homecoming. The American Legion*, the largest First World War veterans' organization, wrote and lobbied successfully for The Adjusted Serviceman's Act of 1944, commonly known as the GI Bill, to ensure history did not repeat itself. Second World War soldiers returned to a society prepared to offer them college tuition, mortgages, business loans, and unemployment compensation while they looked for a civilian job. The GI Bill was the most comprehensive piece of social-welfare legislation in American history, and is rightly celebrated for helping veterans rebuild their civilian lives [84; 93; 94]. Americans, however, rarely remember the GI Bill as the final legacy of the First World War for the nation.

EVOKING THE WAR: REMEMBRANCE AND LESSONS LEARNED

Over time, Americans have forgotten just how important the First World War was to their nation. The physical memorials erected during the period endure, but they no longer evoke the same sorrow. In the 1920s and 1930s, however, the war was anything but forgotten. Most soldiers' families chose to repatriate the bodies of their fallen relatives from France. Commemorating a soldier's death was more than a family affair. Across the nation communities erected doughboy statues in town squares with plaques that bore the names of residents killed. Armistice Day became a national holiday. Tourists flocked to the battlefields, carrying guidebooks that explained the symbolism of the majestic war memorials each Allied government erected [52].

War monuments accented the importance of peace and the horror of the war. In the inter-war period, Americans debated the best way to avoid involvement in future wars. Was it by distancing the country from external conflicts or by taking an activist role in the international arena to diffuse them? Despite the rejection of the Versailles Peace Treaty, the United States did not retreat into isolationism until the 1930s. In the 1920s, disarmament was a popular foreign policy goal once Americans concluded that an arms race was partly responsible for the war. In the 1921–22 Washington Conference, the government negotiated an important naval reduction treaty and a ten-year moratorium on battleship construction with Japan, Great Britain, France, and Italy. To meet the tonnage restrictions, the United States, Britain, and Japan actually reduced the size of existing naval forces. In 1928, the United States joined sixty-two other nations and signed the Kellogg–Briand Pact which renounced war as an offensive instrument of foreign policy.

America's economic power was unchallenged in the 1920s. Should it use this economic power for more than its own enrichment? Could economic clout become a force for peace, or did the drive for profits contribute to war? In the 1920s, Americans were more inclined to accept the first proposition. The wartime trade in armaments and loans had created a favorable balance of trade between the United States and European nations. America shed its previous status as a debtor nation, and became the premier creditor nation in the world [63]. American financiers played a key role in restructuring Germany's reparation payments under the Dawes Plan (1924) and the Young Plan (1929). American banks gave Germany enough money, through loans and investments, to meet the new payment schedule. This money, some of which cycled back to the United States in the form of Allied installments on their war loans, made the European post-war economic recovery heavily dependent on American funds.

In the Depression-plagued 1930s, Americans began to doubt financiers were interested in peace. The Nye Congressional Committee hearings reinforced the widespread conviction that the United States had entered the war to continue profitable arms sales and ensure the Allies repaid their war loans. In response to Hitler's rise to power and the Spanish Civil War,

Americans concluded that the best way to avoid entanglement in another European war was through Neutrality Acts that prohibited the sales of arms, loans, or travel by Americans on the ships of belligerents. These laws limited Roosevelt's ability to aid the Allies during the two years which elapsed between the beginning of the Second World War and the attack on Pearl Harbor [86].

Just as politicians, generals, and soldiers experience war differently, peace presents the international community, the nation, and the individual with unique challenges and opportunities. All desire a just peace, though their definition of this term may differ. After the First World War, however, the world, the nation, and the people shared the nearly unanimous conviction that the peace met few of their expectations. Striving to salvage some good from the war, Americans examined their past mistakes to develop wiser domestic and foreign policies. Whether or not Americans learned the right lessons from the First World War is now a question for students of history to decide.

CHAPTER SIX

THE MEANING OF THE FIRST WORLD WAR FOR THE UNITED STATES

It is not an over-exaggeration to say the First World War was the pivotal event that shaped the twentieth century. Once begun, the war gained a momentum of its own, and try as they might, all participants, from world leaders down to the common soldier, found themselves at the mercy of the war's brutality and the problems it left unresolved. Americans, however, often pass quickly over their own experiences during the war. This is a mistake. During the First World War, Americans wanted to use the war to reform their own society and the world. How well they succeeded or failed in these goals affected the course of American history throughout the century.

How did the war change American society? Wartime conditions created fertile ground for women's suffrage, prohibition, and immigration restrictions. On the other hand, African-American civil rights activists suffered crushing disappointment. Since few African-American soldiers fought, their community never had a chance to use their heroic service record to win increased recognition for civil rights. African-Americans did, however, experience social equality while serving in France and significant numbers of civilians improved their lives by migrating north and taking jobs in wartime industries. It was harder to be an immigrant to the United States after the First World War, but except for German-Americans, the foreign-born discovered that participation in patriotic activities such as liberty loan drives provided an opportunity to assimilate into American society more fully. Progressive reformers educated soldiers about the dangers of venereal disease, thus providing this generation with the first comprehensive sex education program in American history.

Did the government use its power appropriately during the war? During the First World War, a host of federal agencies managed the nation's material and manpower resources. These agencies employed a range of tactics, including patriotic appeals to conserve resources, loaning money to co-operative businesses, and seizing control of the railroads. Overall, the government formed a mostly cooperative regulatory relationship with business. In the 1920s, many Americans accepted this ongoing government–business partnership as a modern, moderate alternative to the previous *laissez-faire* free market system or the Progressive preference for strict government regulation. The wartime coalition, however, included a place for labor. The post-war collaboration between the government and business did not. To the dismay of workers, the government abandoned its wartime guarantee of labor's right to organize unions and to collective bargaining.

Justice Department enforcement of the Espionage and Sedition Acts, and investigations during the First Red Scare of 1919, diluted Americans' right to freedom of speech and assembly. The Supreme Court established a 'clear and present danger' test that made these rights contingent on circumstances, rather than absolute. Taking their cue from the government, private citizens felt free to take matters into their own hands when they determined certain groups were disrupting the unity of spirit and action required to win the war. The government's call for all citizens to support the war whole-heartedly and its prosecution of pacifists and radicals fostered hysterical distrust of any who opposed the war. The government had a responsibility to protect the country from German sabotage, but in the process unleashed passions that were difficult to contain.

Did the war make the United States a world power? Americans came to believe their involvement in the war was critical, both to win it for the Allies and to make the world safe for democracy. Within an amazingly short amount of time, the nation mobilized four million men and sent two million overseas. The unending wave of American troops arriving from overseas convinced a demoralized German government to sue for peace. In fighting the war, Pershing's insistence on leading an independent American army in the field overshadowed how often the Americans cooperated and compromised with the British and the French. In similar fashion, the country's rejection of the Versailles Treaty and its refusal to join the League of Nations signaled to many observers an American retreat into isolationism. The conclusion that Americans went their own way after the war slights the strong economic relationship the United States maintained with Europe and the country's efforts in the 1920s to ensure collective security through disarmament and anti-war pacts. It was the Depression, not rejection of the Versailles Treaty, which caused the United States to turn inward and to focus primarily on domestic problems.

Was the First World War a just war for the United States? This is the hardest question to answer because definitions of just war vary tremendously. Was the United States rightly defending itself against German threats to its commerce on the high seas and along its South West border, or had the United States forced Germany to take these extreme positions by accepting the British blockade? Were clear national interests at stake for the United

States during the war? Wilson told the American people that they had the moral responsibility to enter the war since they were the only power capable of establishing a just and lasting peace. This definition of just war required more than a good reason for fighting the war, it demanded a just peace settlement.

Conclusions about the country's mistakes during the First World War influenced how America reacted to the Second World War. Americans first passed Neutrality Acts to prevent a profitable arms trade from drawing the United States into the war. Then, once in the war, demanded unconditional surrender to avoid the ambiguity of an Armistice. In the aftermath of the Second World War, Americans retained their earlier fear of communism but this time the country resolved to provide world leadership in foreign affairs and to join the United Nations. Later in the century Americans lamented because the Korean and Vietnam Wars barely resembled the Second World War. The Second World War, however, was perhaps the most atypical of all of America's twentieth-century wars. In many respects, the questions raised about just war and America's world position in the 1950s and 1960s recalled the dilemmas Americans confronted during the First World War. The First World War therefore was the first, but not the last, war to shape the American nation in the twentieth century.

On 7 May 1915, a German submarine sunk a British passenger ship, the Lusitania, *killing 128 Americans. Eventually, the German government expressed regret over the loss of American lives. The following 19 May 1915 editorial from a German-American newspaper,* Fatherland, *argued that Germany's act was justified. Few mainstream newspapers agreed, instead they overwhelmingly condemned Germany for the attack. Though the United States was a neutral nation when German-Americans expressed this support for Germany, once America entered the war many Americans viewed these earlier statements as evidence that they were traitors or disloyal to the United States.*

Legally and morally there is no basis for any protest on the part of the United States. The *Lusitania* was a British ship. British ships have been instructed by the Admiralty to ram submarines and to take active measures against the enemy. Hence every British ship must be considered in the light of a warship.

The *Lusitania* flew the ensign of the British Naval Reserves before the submarine warfare was initiated. Since that time she has hoisted many a flag, including the Stars and Stripes. According to a statement issued by the advertising manager of the Cunard Line, the *Lusitania* 'when torpedoed was entirely out of the control of the Cunard Company and operated under the command of the British Admiralty.'

The *Lusitania* carried contraband of war from this country to England. If this contraband had reached its destination it would undoubtedly have killed far more Germans than the total number of passengers lost on the *Lusitania*. As a matter of fact it did actually kill the passengers by precipitating the sinking of the ship. There can be no doubt that the ship would not have sunk for hours, if explosions from within had not hastened its end. *Every passenger on a boat carrying contraband of war takes his life into his hands.* The explosives in the hold of a ship, we repeat, constitutes a graver peril to passengers than the shots of German torpedoes. It cannot be said that the *Lusitania* was torpedoed without warning. Ordinarily a half hour's warning is regarded sufficient. In this case the ship was warned of its fate *four or five days in advance.* We need only turn to the warning notice issued by the German Embassy on the day before the *Lusitania* left the harbor of New York.

[This statement refers to the warning that the German Embassy placed in American newspapers on 1 May 1915. Secretary of State William Jennings Bryan approved the advertisement after German officials told him the *Lusitania* was carrying ammunition. The advertisement actually appeared on the day that the *Lusitania* set sail and stated: 'TRAVELLERS [*sic*] intending to embark on the Atlantic voyage are reminded that a state of war exists between Germany and her allies and Great Britain and her allies; that the zone of war includes the waters adjacent to the British Isles; that in accordance with formal notice given by the Imperial German Government, vessels flying the flag of Great Britain, or of any of her allies, are liable to destruction in those waters and that travellers sailing in the war zone on ships of Great Britain or her allies do so at their own risk.']

Instead of urging the President to take steps against Germany, we should impeach the Secretary of State for his neglect of duty in not warning all Americans of the peril of ocean traffic in the war zone, especially under the flag of a belligerent nation. If the Secretary of State ... had issued such a warning, not a single American life would have been forfeited. Germany, provoked by England which established a war zone as early as November [1914] and made the importation of foodstuffs into Germany practically impossible, decided upon submarine warfare as a measure of retaliation. She was forced to do so by the signal failure of the United States to protect the common rights of neutrals. When Germany determines upon a plan of action she means business. The Germans are not a nation of poker players. Germany does not bluff.

The sinking of the *Lusitania* is a terrific lesson, but in order to drive home its force more fully and to safeguard this country from further losses and from the danger of complications with Germany, the State Department should issue at once a formal notice admonishing American citizens to shun all ships flying the flag of a belligerent nation and all ships, *irrespective of nationality*, which carry across the sea the tools of destruction.

W. Dudley, [7], pp. 82–4.

DOCUMENT 2   PRESIDENT WOODROW WILSON'S WAR ADDRESS

The Congressmen who assembled to hear Wilson address them on 2 April 1917 did not know until the middle of his speech that the President, who had sought numerous diplomatic solutions, had come to ask them for a declaration of war against Germany. In this excerpt from the address, Wilson describes the war as a crusade for democracy.

We have no quarrel with the German people. We have no feeling toward them but one of sympathy and friendship. It was not upon their impulse that their government acted in entering this war. It was not with their previous knowledge or approval. It was a war determined upon as wars used to be determined upon in the old, unhappy days when peoples were nowhere consulted by their rulers and wars were provoked and waged in the interest of dynasties or of little groups of ambitious men who were accustomed to use their fellow men as pawns and tools. ...

We are accepting this challenge of hostile purpose because we know that in such a government, following such methods, we can never have a friend; and that in the presence of its organized power, always lying in wait to accomplish we know not what purpose, there can be no assured security for the democratic governments of the world. We are now about to accept gauge of battle with this natural foe to liberty and shall, if necessary, spend the whole force of the nation to check and nullify its pretensions and its power. We are glad, now that we see the facts with no veil of false pretense about them, to fight thus for the ultimate peace of the world and for the liberation of its peoples, the German peoples included: for the rights of nations great and small and the privilege of men everywhere to chose their way of life and of obedience. The world must be made safe for democracy. Its peace must be planted upon the tested foundations of political liberty. We have no selfish ends to serve. We desire no conquest, no dominion. We seek no indemnities for ourselves, no material compensation for the sacrifices we shall freely make. We are but one of the champions of the rights of mankind. We shall be satisfied when those rights have been made as secure as the faith and the freedom of nations can make them. ...

It is a distressing and oppressive duty, Gentlemen of the Congress, which I have performed in thus addressing you. There are, it may be, many months of fiery trial and sacrifice ahead of us. It is a fearful thing to lead this great peaceful people into war, into the most terrible and disastrous of all wars, civilization itself seeming to be in the balance. But the right is more precious than peace, and we shall fight for the things which we have always carried nearest our hearts, for democracy, for the right of those who submit to authority to have a voice in their own governments, for the rights and liberties of small nations, for a universal dominion of right by such a concert of free peoples as shall bring peace and safety to all nations and make the world itself at last free. To such a task we can dedicate our lives and our fortunes, everything that we are and everything that we have, with the pride of those who know that the day has come when America is privileged to spend her blood and her might for the principles that gave her birth and happiness and the peace which she has treasured. God helping her, she can do no other.

O. L. Graham, Jr., [162], pp. 330–2.

DOCUMENT 3   THE FOURTEEN POINTS

On 8 January 1918, Wilson outlined the following program to establish a just peace. There were important differences between the ideals Wilson outlined and the goals of France and Britain, differences which became apparent at the Paris Peace Conference in 1919.

We entered this war because violations of right had occurred which touched us to the quick and made the life of our own people impossible unless they were corrected and the world secured once for all against their recurrence. What we demand in this war, therefore, is nothing peculiar to ourselves. It is that the world be made fit and safe to live in; and particularly that it be made safe for every peace-loving nation which, like our own, wishes to live its own life, determine its own institutions, be assured of justice and fair dealing by the other peoples of the world as against force and selfish aggression. All the peoples of the world are in effect partners in this interest, and for our own part we see very clearly that unless justice be done to others it will not be done to us. The program of the world's peace, therefore, is our program; and that program, the only possible program, as we see it, is this:

I.   Open covenants of peace, openly arrived at, after which there shall be no private international understandings of any kind but diplomacy shall proceed always frankly and in the public view.

II. Absolute freedom of navigation upon the seas, outside territorial waters, alike in peace and in war, except as the seas may be closed in whole or in part by international action for the enforcement of international covenants.

III. The removal, so far as possible, of all economic barriers and the establishment of an equality of trade conditions among all the nations consenting to the peace and associating themselves for its maintenance.

IV. Adequate guarantees given and taken that national armaments will be reduced to the lowest point consistent with domestic safety.

V.   A free, open-minded, and absolutely impartial adjustment of all colonial claims, based upon a strict observance of the principle that in determining all such questions of sovereignty the interests of the populations concerned must have equal weight with the equitable claims of the government whose title is to be determined.

VI. The evacuation of all Russian territory and such a settlement of all questions affecting Russia as will secure the best and freest cooperation of the other nations of the world in obtaining for her an unhampered and unembarrassed opportunity for the independent determination of her own political development and national policy and assure her of a sincere welcome into the society of free nations under institutions of her own choosing; and, more than a welcome, assistance also of every kind that she may need and may herself desire. The treatment accorded Russia by her sister nations in the months to come will be the acid test of their good will, of their comprehension of her needs as distinguished from their own interests, and of their intelligent and unselfish sympathy.

VII. Belgium, the whole world will agree, must be evacuated and restored, without any attempt to limit the sovereignty which she enjoys in common with all other free nations. No other single act will serve as this will serve to restore confidence among the nations in the laws which they have themselves set and determined for the government of their relations with one another. Without this healing act the whole structure and validity of international law is forever impaired.

VIII. All French territory should be freed and the invaded portions restored, and the wrong done to France by Prussia in 1871 in the matter of Alsace-Lorraine, which has unsettled the peace of the world for nearly fifty years, should be righted, in order that peace may once more be made secure in the interest of all.

IX. A readjustment of the frontiers of Italy should be effected along clearly recognizable lines of nationality.

X. The peoples of Austria-Hungary, whose place among the nations we wish to see safeguarded and assured, should be accorded the freest opportunity of autonomous development.

XI. Rumania, Serbia, and Montenegro should be evacuated; occupied territories restored; Serbia accorded free and secure access to the sea; and the relations of the several Balkan states to one another determined by friendly counsel along historically established lines of allegiance and nationality; and international guarantees of the political and economic independence and territorial integrity of the several Balkan states should be entered into.

XII. The Turkish portions of the present Ottoman empire should be assured a secure sovereignty, but the other nationalities which are now under Turkish rule should be assured an undoubted security of life and an absolutely unmolested opportunity of autonomous development, and the Dardanelles should be permanently opened as a free passage to the ships and commerce of all nations under international guarantees.

XIII. An independent Polish state should be erected which should include the territories inhabited by indisputably Polish populations, which should be assured a free and secure access to the sea, and whose political and economic independence and territorial integrity should be guaranteed by international covenant.

XIV. A general association of nations must be formed under specific covenants for the purpose of affording mutual guarantees of political independence and territorial integrity to great and small states alike. ...

An evident principle runs through the whole program I have outlined. It is the principle of justice to all peoples and nationalities, and their right to live on equal terms of liberty and safety with one another, whether they be strong or weak. Unless this principle be made its foundation no part of the structure of international justice can stand. The people of the United States could act upon no other principle; and to the vindication of this principle they are ready to devote their lives, their honor, and everything that they possess. The moral climax of this the culminating and final war for human liberty has come, and they are ready to put their own strength, their own highest purpose, their own integrity and devotion to the test.

A. Link (ed.), [8], pp. 534–9.

DOCUMENT 4   PSYCHOLOGICAL EXAMINATIONS IN THE UNITED STATES ARMY

The following examples are taken from the intelligence tests given to American soldiers in domestic training camps. Psychologists claimed that they measured ability and concluded that the average American soldier had a mental age of thirteen. Rather than intelligence, many test questions measured familiarity with mainstream American culture and the level of schooling.

These questions were included in the Alpha exam given to literate recruits. The underlined word or checked box was considered the correct response.

6 **Food** products are made by ☐Smith & Wesson ☐<u>Swift & Co.</u> ☐W. L. Douglas ☐B. T. Babbitt

10 'Hasn't **scratched yet**' is used in advertising a ☐duster ☐flour ☐brush <u>cleanser</u>

17 **Nabisco** is a ☐patent medicine ☐disinfectant ☐<u>food product</u> ☐tooth paste

21 The **dictaphone** is a kind of ☐typewriter ☐multigraph ☐<u>phonograph</u> ☐adding machine

25 The **Battle of Gettysburg** was fought in ☐<u>1863</u> ☐1813 ☐1778 ☐1812

32 **Spare** is a term used in ☐<u>bowling</u> ☐football ☐tennis ☐hockey

40 **Scrooge** appears in ☐Vanity Fair ☐<u>The Christmas Carol</u> ☐Romola ☐Henry IV

---

2 Why are pencils more commonly carried than fountain pens? Because

☒ they are brightly colored

☐ they are cheaper

☐ they are not so heavy

3 Why is leather used for shoes? Because

☐ it is produced in all countries

☒ it wears well

☐ it is an animal product

6   Streets are sprinkled in summer
    ☐ to make the air cooler
    ☐ to keep automobiles from skidding
    ☒ to keep down dust

7   Why is wheat better food than corn? Because
    ☒ it is more nutritious
    ☐ it is more expensive
    ☐ it can be ground finer

8   If a man made a million dollars he ought to
    ☐ pay off the national debt
    ☒ contribute to various worthy charities
    ☐ give it all to some poor man

The Beta exam was a pictorial intelligence test given to illiterates and non-English speaking soldiers. These were the instructions for examiners preparing soldiers for the maze test.

It is most important that examination beta be given in a genial manner. The subjects who take this examination sometimes sulk and refuse to work. ... [To show soldiers how to take the exam, the] demonstrator makes one mistake by going into the blind alley at upper left-hand corner of maze. Examiner apparently does not notice what demonstrator is doing until he crosses line at end of alley; then examiner shakes his head vigorously, says 'No-no,' takes demonstrator's hand and traces back to the place where he may start right again. Demonstrator traces rest of maze so as to indicate an attempt at haste, hesitating only at ambiguous points. Examiner says 'Good.' Then holding up blank, 'Look here,' and draws an imaginary line across the page from left to right for every maze on the page. Then, 'All right. Go ahead. Do it (pointing to men and then to books). Hurry up.' The idea of working fast must be impressed on the men during the maze test. Examiner and orderlies walk around the room, motioning to men who are not working, and saying, 'Do it, do it, hurry up, quick.' At the end of 2 minutes examiner says, 'Stop! ...'

Memoirs of the National Academy of Sciences, Vol. XV, Government Printing Office, Washington, DC, 1921, pp. 163, 164, 222, 227, 251, 256

DOCUMENT 5   WAR BOND POSTER; ESPIONAGE AND SEDITION ACTS

This war bond poster exaggerated the physical threat to the United States and stereotyped the German enemy as a vicious Hun to encourage Americans to purchase war bonds and support the war. Images like these created problems for German-Americans whose loyalty was called into question. During the war, the government was less interested in protecting the right to free speech and freedom of assembly and more intent on using the Espionage (1917) and Sedition (1918) Acts, excerpted below, to stop dissent and treason.

THE ESPIONAGE ACT of 15 June 1917

Title I, Section 3
Whoever, when the United States is at war, shall willfully make or convey false reports or false statements with intent to interfere with the operation or success of the military or naval forces of the United States or to promote the success of its enemies and whoever, when the United States is at war, shall willfully cause or attempt to cause insubordination, disloyalty, mutiny, or refusal of duty, in the military or naval forces of the United States, or shall willfully obstruct the recruiting or enlistment service of the United States, to the injury of the service of the United States, shall be punished by a fine of not more than $10,000 or imprisonment for not more than twenty years, or both.

Title XII, Section 2
Every letter, writing, circular, postal card, picture, print, engraving, photograph, newspaper, pamphlet, book, or other publication, matter, or thing, of any kind, containing any matter advocating or urging treason, insurrection, or forcible resistance to any law of the United States, is hereby declared to be nonmailable.

THE SEDITION ACT of 16 May 1918

Be it enacted by the Senate and House of Representatives of the United States of America in Congress assembled, That section three of title one of the Act entitled 'An Act to punish acts of interference with the foreign relations, the neutrality, and the foreign commerce of the United States, to punish espionage, and better to enforce the criminal laws of the United States, and for other purposes,' approved June fifteenth, nineteen hundred and seventeen, be, and the same is hereby amended so as to read as follows: 'Sec. 3. Whoever, when the United States is at war, shall willfully make or convey false reports or false statements with intent to interfere with the operation or success of the military or naval forces of the United States, or to promote the success of its enemies, or shall willfully make or convey false reports or false statements, or say or do anything except by way of bona fide and not disloyal advice to an investor or investors, with intent to obstruct the sale by the United States of bonds or other securities of the United States or the making of loans by or to the United States, and whoever, when the United States is at war, shall willfully cause or attempt to cause, or incite or attempt to incite, insubordination, disloyalty, mutiny, or refusal of duty, in the military or naval forces of the United States, or shall willfully obstruct or attempt to obstruct the recruiting or enlistment service of the United States, and whoever, when the United States is at war, shall willfully utter, print, write, or publish any disloyal, profane, scurrilous, or abusive language about the form of government of the United States, or the Constitution of the United States, or the military or naval forces of the United States, or the flag of the United States, or the uniform of the Army or Navy of the United States, or any language intended to bring the form of government of the United States, or the Constitution of the United States, or the military or naval forces of the United States, or the flag of the United States, or the uniform of the Army or Navy of the United States to come into contempt, scorn, contumely, or disrepute, or shall willfully utter, print, write, or publish any language intended to incite, provoke, or encourage resistance to the United States, or to promote the cause of its enemies, or shall willfully display the flag of any foreign enemy, or shall willfully by utterance, writing, printing, publication, or language spoken, urge, incite, or advocate any curtailment of production in this country of any thing or things, product or products, necessary or essential to the prosecution of the war in which the United States may be engaged, with intent by such curtailment to cripple or hinder the United States in the prosecution of the war, and whoever shall willfully advocate, teach, defend, or suggest the doing of any of the acts or things in this section enumerated, and whoever shall by word or act support or favor the cause of any country with which the United States is at war or by word or act oppose the cause of the United States therein, shall be punished by a fine of not more than $10,000 or imprisonment for not more than twenty years, or both: Provided, That any employee or official of the United States Government who commits any disloyal act or utters any unpatriotic or disloyal language, or who, in an abusive and violent manner criticizes the Army or Navy or the flag of the United States shall be at once dismissed from the service. Any such employee shall be dismissed by the head of the department in which the employee may be engaged, and any such official shall be dismissed by the authority having power to appoint a successor to the dismissed official.

War bond poster: By F. Strothmann, the National Archives. Reproduced in E. J. Gorn, R. Roberts, T. D. Bilhartz, *Constructing the American Past: A Source Book of a People's History*, HarperCollins, New York, 1995, p. 189. Espionage and Sedition Acts: R. Schaffer, [82], pp. 218–21.

DOCUMENT 6	CLOSE RANKS

In this controversial editorial, W. E. B. Du Bois urges African-Americans to support the war. It took twenty years before Du Bois agreed with those who believed African-Americans should demand recognition of their civil rights before supporting the war.

This is the crisis of the world. For all the long years to come men will point to the year 1918 as the great Day of Decision, the day when the world decided whether it would submit to military despotism and an endless armed peace – if peace it could be called – or whether they would put down the menace of German militarism and inaugurate the United States of the World.

We of the colored race have no ordinary interest in the outcome. That which the German power represents today spells death to the aspirations of Negroes and all darker races for equality, freedom and democracy. Let us not hesitate. Let us, while this war lasts, forget our special grievances and close our ranks shoulder to shoulder with our own white fellow citizens and the allied nations that are fighting for democracy. We make no ordinary sacrifice but we make it gladly and willingly with our eyes lifted to the hills.

The Crisis, 16 July 1918, p. 111.

DOCUMENT 7   A BLACK SERGEANT'S LETTER

In this May 1919 letter to civil rights activist W. E. B. Du Bois, veteran Charles Isum contrasts his encounters with racist white American soldiers with the warm welcome that he received from French civilians.

Dear Sir,

I have just finished reading the May issue of the CRISIS and have enjoyed it immensely. I am indeed pleased to note that someone has the nerve and backbone to tell the public the unvarnished facts concerning the injustice, discrimination and southern prejudices practiced by the white Americans against the black Americans in France.

I am a recently discharged Sergeant of the Medical Detachment, 365th. Infantry, 92nd.Division, and I take this opportunity to relate one of my personal experiences with the southern rednecks who were in command of my division, brigade and regiment.

On or about December 26, 1918 General Order No. 40 was issued from the headquarters of the 92nd.Division. I cannot recall the exact wording of the part of the order which was of a discriminating nature, but it read something to this effect, 'Military Police will see that soldiers do not address, carry on conversation with or accompany the female inhabitants of this area'. At the time this order was issued we were billeted in the village of Ambrieres, Mayenne. There were white soldiers also billeted in the same village but they did not belong to the 92nd.Division and the order did not affect them, hence it was an order for Colored soldiers only. It was not an A.E.F. order. It was a divisional order for Colored soldiers. We were living in the same houses with the French people and under the terms of this order we were forbidden to even speak to the people with whom we lived, while the white soldiers of the 325th.Baking Co. and the Subsupply Depot #10 were allowed to address, visit or accompany these same people where and whenever they desired.

On Jan. 21, 1919 Mademoiselle Marie Meziere, the eldest daughter of Monsieur Charles Meziere, a merchant tailor of Ambieres [*sic*] was married to Monsieur Maurice Barbe, a French soldier. I was invited to be a guest at the wine party, to accompany the bridal party on the marriage promenade and to be a guest at the supper, which was to take place at 8:30 p.m. I attended the party with a few other Colored soldiers from the Medical Detachment. No whites were invited but Capt. Willis (white) of the Supply Company butted in. He spoke miserable french [*sic*] and the members of the party called on the Colored soldiers to interpret for him. Willis became enraged and turned his back on the Colored boys and told the French people that it was improper for them to associate with the black soldiers. The French people paid no attention to what he said and we all left him sitting in the cafe alone. His temperature at this time was about 104 degrees. The other Colored soldiers returned to the Infirmary and I accompanied the bridal party on the promenade out on the boulevard. There were seven persons in the party; the bride and groom, the bride's sister, the groom's brother and sister, a French soldier and myself. I was the only American. As we reached town on returning from the stroll Colonel George McMaster, Commanding Officer of our regiment accosted me and demanded, 'Who are you. What are you doing with these people' I told him and he called a Military Police and ordered me taken to the Adjutant with orders for the Adjutant to prefer charges against me for accompanying white people. On arriving at the Adjutant's hotel we found Capt. Willis there evidently waiting for me to be brought in. The Adjutant only asked two questions, 'Was he with a girl?' 'What is your name and to what company do you belong?'. Then he said, 'Put him in the guard house.'

The following afternoon I was ordered to appear for trial. At 1:15 p.m. I was taken through the streets to the Town Mayor's office by an armed guard who was a private soldier – my rank was not respected. I was called into the room and was surprised to find there there [*sic*] was no one present but Major Paul Murry. He read the charges which had me charged with violating the 96th. Article of War and with disobeying General Order No. 40. After reading the charges he asked for my plea. I told him that I did not care to plea that I would exercise my right as a non-commissioned to refuse trial in a Summary Court. This was a complete surprise to him. He had no idea that I was aware of my rights. He looked it up in the Manual of Army Court Martials and said that it was my right but I was very foolish to use it. I told him that from the appearance of things there had been no intention of giving me a fair trial. The prosecuting witness was not present, the members of the board were absent and I had not been given an opportunity to call witness or secure counsel. At first he tried to frighten and intimidate me by saying that if I were given a General Court Martial trial I would be left in France awaiting trial after my regiment had gone home. He also said that I might get six months in Leavenworth if I should be found guilty. (Can you imagine it – six months for walking on the street with white people.) After he saw he could not intimidate me he assumed the air of comradship [*sic*] and used all his presusaive [*sic*] powers to intice [*sic*] me to submit to a speedy quiet trial in his kangaroo court but I stood pat. He said that I was trying to play martyr and was trying to make a big fuss out of a little incident, but I claimed that I was standing for a principle, that I had been unjustly treated, that the G.O. was unconstitutional, undemocratic and in direct opposition to the principles for which we had fought. I asked that General Pershing be given a copy of the General Order and also a copy of the charges against me. He laughed at this request and said that the General was too busy for such small matters. He gave me a half an hour to think the matter over and stated that I might get some advice from the officers present. There were only two present. They had come in during the argument. One was Capt. Willis and the other Capt. Benj. Thomas. I took the matter up with Capt. Thomas and in the meantime my Detachment Commander, Major E. B. Simmons (white), of Massachusetts came in and I told him my story. He became indignant and told me to fight it to the last ditch and he would do all in his power to help me. I returned to the court room, and demanded a General Court Martial Trial and a release from the guard house pending trial. Major Murry said that I was making a great mistake and reluctantly gave me a release from the guard house.

That night I visited some of my French friends and found that the whole town was in an uproar over my case. M. Meziere had been to prevail on the Town Mayor in my behalf and was informed that nothing could be done and the Americans had charge of the town. M. Meziere had also called on Brig. Gen. Gehardt our Brigade Commander, another Negro-hater of the meanest type. He refused to even give M. Meziere a civil audience. M. Meziere then went to the Town Mayor and swore to an affidavit that my character was of the best, that I was a respected friend of the family and was their invited guest. Mme. Emil Harmon, my landlady also made an affidavit of character in my behalf (I now have both affidavits in my possession).

The following day I was rearrested at my billet and placed in the guard house, contrary to military rules. The Manual of Army Court Martials states that a non-commissioned officer shall not be confined in a guard house with privates but no attention was paid to that rule. No charges were given and no explanation made except that it was Colonel McMaster's orders. I was released that night and sent to my Detachment under 'arrest in quarters'. Nothing more has been said about the case to this day except at New York when I asked Major Murry when I was going to have my trial and he said that the best thing to do was to keep quiet about it.

On March 22, 1919 I was given an honorable discharge from the army, with character grade Excellent and rank of Sergeant M.D. No mention of the case was made on my Service Record. If I had committed an offense sufficient to cause me to be arrested twice and placed in the guard house, why was I given an honorable discharge with and [*sic*] Excellent grade character and a non-commissioned officer's rank?

If space would permit I could quote other instances where our boys were shamefully mistreated by the white Americans while in France.

> Respectfully yours,
> Charles R. Isum
> Formerly Sergeant Medical Detachment, 365th.Inf.

W. E. B. Du Bois Papers, University of Massachusetts-Amherst, microfilm reel 7, frame 980.

DOCUMENT 8   FACTS AND QUESTIONS CONCERNING THE NREF

A severe morale crisis swept through the American forces stationed in North Russia (the North Russia Expeditionary Force) in 1919. Stranded in the ice-locked area until spring, this soldier petition written in February protests the American involvement in the Russian revolution and illustrates the reasons President Wilson eventually withdrew troops in June.

1. We officers enlisted and our men were drafted for the purpose of fighting Germany and her allies.
2. This force was sent to Russia to prevent Germany from establishing naval bases in the far North.
3. The American organisations have been split up and placed under British officers. England has undoubtedly many capable officers, but they are not in Russia. However we, ourselves, are woefully lacking in that respect. The manner in which this expedition has been mishandled is a disgrace to the civilized world.
4. Our original purpose having been accomplished we are now meddling with a Russian revolution and counter-revolution.
5. Is this consistent with the principles of American democracy?
6. The majority of the people here seem to prefer Bolshevism to British intervention. They mistrust the British. It is our opinion that British diplomats pulled the wool over the eyes of our representatives, to the end that we were sent with this expedition in an effort to take the curse off the British.
7. The few French here finally rebelled against British rule and have been given a French commander.

8. WHERE IS OUR MONROE DOCTRINE?
   If we stood by, while Mexico was torn by revolutions, the sanctity of our borders violated and Americans murdered, on what basis is our presence here justified? A British officer here, who is more human than most, quite aptly described this expedition as an effort to put on a show with two men and an orange.

9. We are fighting against enormous odds in men, artillery and material. Most of the men in the enemy forces have seen years of service. If they were not lacking in morale and discipline, we should have been wiped off the face of the earth ere this.

10. Due to a pending election in England, and the fear of antagonizing the labor parties, no reenforcements [*sic*] have been sent out. In fact before the election, certain British officials placed themselves on record as having no intentions [*sic*] of sending more troops to Russia.

11. We wonder what propaganda is at work in the States, which enables the War Department to keep troops here. It seems to us as though it is a question of potential dollars in Russia.

12. We, a porition [*sic*] of the civilian army of America, organized to fight Germany, wonder why we are called upon to spend American lives aiding and abetting a counter-revolution in Russia while the great majority of the people here sit idly by watching the show, not idly either, for the [*sic*] most of the natives here are Bolshevists in sympathy. We have no heart in the fight. We are fighting neither for Russia or for Russian wealth but for our lives. We have earnestly endeavored to find some justification for our being here, but have been unable to reconcile this expedition with American ideals and principles instilled within us.

13. We are removed 200 miles from our base, with an open country intervening, with no force except in a few villages to guard our lines and with the enemy within striking distance of the line. There is no military reason why we should be more than 20 miles from our base.

[Note from officer who confiscated the pamphlet:] The above was written by an American officer with the Dvina force and it is reported that it is widely circulated among the American troops at the front and the men consider that it fully covers their ideas regarding the reasons why American troops are kept here.

National Archives, Washington, DC, Textual Records of the War Department General & Special Staffs, Record Group 165; Office of the Director of Intelligence (G–2), 1906–49; Security Classified Correspondence and Reports, 1917–41 (Entry 65); file # 24–327(59).

DOCUMENT 9   SENATOR HENRY CABOT LODGE OPPOSES THE VERSAILLES TREATY

At the Peace Conference, Wilson made numerous compromises to gain Allied support for a League of Nations where disputes would be settled peacefully. Republican Senator, Henry Cabot Lodge, raises key objections about America joining the League of Nations in these following excerpts taken from his 12 August 1919 address to Congress. Lodge contends that the League Covenant strips Congress of its power to declare war, that joining the League represented a fundamental shift in American foreign policy, and suggests that joining the League will hamper the process of Americanizing immigrants.

If Europe desires such an alliance or league with a power of this kind, then so be it. ... But I object in the strongest possible way to having the United States agree, directly or indirectly, to be controlled by a league which may at any time, and perfectly lawfully and in accordance with the terms of the covenant, be drawn in to deal with the internal conflicts in other countries, no matter what those conflicts may be. We should never permit the United States to be involved in the internal conflict in another country, except by the will of her people expressed through the Congress which represents them.

With regard to wars of external aggression on a member of the league, the case is perfectly clear. There can be no genuine dispute whatever about the meaning of the first clause of article 10. In the first place, it differs from every other obligation in being individual and placed upon each nation without the intervention of the league. Each nation for itself promises to respect and preserve as against external aggression the boundaries and the political independence of every member of the league. ...

It is, I repeat, an individual obligation. It requires no action on the part of the league, except that in the second sentence the authorities of the league are to have the power to advise as to the means to be employed in order to fulfill the purpose of the first sentence. But that is a detail of execution, and I consider that we are morally and in honor bound to accept and act upon that advice. The broad fact remains that if any member of the league suffering from external aggression should appeal directly to the United States for support the United States would be bound to give that support in its own capacity and without reference to the action of other powers, because the United States itself is bound, and I hope the day will never come when the United States will not carry out its promises. If that day should come, and the United States or any other great country should refuse, no matter how specious the reasons, to fulfill both in letter and spirit every obligation in this covenant, the United States would be dishonored and the league would crumble into dust, leaving behind it a legacy of wars. If China should rise up and attack Japan in an effort to undo the great wrong of the cession of the control of Shantung to that power, we should be bound under the terms of article 10 to sustain Japan against China, and a guaranty of that sort is never involved except when the question has passed beyond the stage of negotiation and has become a question for the application of force. I do not like the prospect. It shall not come into existence by any vote of mine. ...

Those of us, Mr. President [of the Senate], who are either wholly opposed to the league, or who are trying to preserve the independence and the safety of the United States by changing the terms of the league, and who are endeavoring to make the league, if we are to be a member of it, less certain to promote war instead of peace have been reproached with selfishness in our outlook and with a desire to keep our country in a state of isolation. So far as the question of isolation goes, it is impossible to isolate the United States. I well remember the time, 20 years ago, when eminent Senators and other distinguished gentlemen who were opposing the Philippines and shrieking about imperialism sneered at the statement made by some of us, that the United States had become a world power. I think no one now would question that the Spanish war marked the entrance of the United States into world affairs to a degree which had never obtained before. It was both an inevitable and an irrevocable step, and our entrance into the war with Germany certainly showed once and for all that the United States was not unmindful of its world responsibilities. We may set aside all this empty talk about isolation. Nobody expects to isolate the United States or to make it a hermit Nation, which is a sheer absurdity. But there is a wide difference between taking a suitable part and bearing a due responsibility in world affairs and plunging the United States into every controversy and conflict on the face of the globe. By meddling in all the differences which may arise among any portion or fragment of humankind we simply fritter away our influence and injure ourselves to no good purpose. We shall be of far more value to the world and its peace by occupying, so far as possible, the situation which we have occupied for the last 20 years and by adhering to the policy of [George] Washington and [Alexander] Hamilton, of [Thomas] Jefferson and [James] Monroe, under which we have risen to our present greatness and prosperity. The fact that we have been separated by our geographical situation and by our consistent policy from the broils of Europe has made us more than any one thing capable of performing the great work which we performed in the war against Germany and our disinterestedness is of far more value to the world than our eternal meddling in every possible dispute could ever be.

Now, as to our selfishness, I have no desire to boast that we are better than our neighbors, but the fact remains that this Nation in making peace with Germany had not a single selfish or individual interest to serve. All we asked was that Germany should be rendered incapable of again breaking forth, with all the horrors, incident to German warfare, upon an unoffending world, and that demand was shared by every free nation and indeed by humanity itself. For ourselves we asked absolutely nothing. We have not asked any government or governments to guarantee our boundaries or our political independence. We have no fear in regard to either. We have sought no territory, no privileges, no advantages, for ourselves. That is the fact. It is apparent on the face of the treaty. I do not mean to reflect upon a single one of the powers with which we have been associated in the war against Germany, but there is not one of them which has not sought individual advantages for their own national benefit. I do not criticize their desires at all. The services and sacrifices of England and France and Belgium and Italy are beyond estimate and beyond praise. I am glad they should have what they desire for their own welfare and safety. But they all receive under the peace territorial and commercial benefits. We are asked to give, and we in no way seek to take. Surely it is not too much to insist that when we are offered nothing but the opportunity to give and to aid others we should have the right to say what sacrifices we shall make and what the magnitude of our gifts shall be. In the prosecution of the war we gave unstintedly American lives and American treasure. When the war closed we had 3,000,000 men under arms. We were turning the country into a vast workshop for war. We advanced ten billions to our allies. We refused no assistance that we could possibly render. All the great energy and power of the Republic were put at the service of the good cause. We have not been ungenerous. We have been devoted to the cause of freedom, humanity, and civilization everywhere. Now we are asked, in the making of peace, to sacrifice our sovereignty in important respects, to involve ourselves almost without limit in the affairs of other nations and to yield up policies and rights which we have maintained throughout our history. We are asked to incur liabilities to an unlimited extent and furnish assets at the same time which no man can measure. I think it is not only our right but our duty to determine how far we shall go. Not only must we look carefully to see where we are being led into endless disputes and entanglements, but we must not forget that we have in this country millions of people of foreign birth and parentage.

Our one great object is to make all these people Americans so that we may call on them to place America first and serve America as they have done in the war just closed. We cannot Americanize them if we are continually thrusting them back into the quarrels and difficulties of the countries from which they came to us. We shall fill this land with political disputes about the troubles and quarrels of other countries. We shall have a large portion of our people voting not on American questions and not on what concerns the United States but dividing on issues which concern foreign countries alone. That is an unwholesome and perilous condition to force upon this country. We must avoid it.

Congressional Record, 66th Congress, 1st Session, pp. 3778–84.

This speech, on 25 September 1919, in Pueblo, Colorado, was the last one that Wilson gave in defense of the League of Nations before suffering the stroke which left him sick and weak for the rest of his term.

But you will say, 'what is the second sentence of article 10? That is what gives very disturbing thoughts.' The second sentence is that the Council of the League shall advise what steps, if any, are necessary to carry out the guaranty of the first sentence, namely, that the members will respect and preserve the territorial integrity and political independence of the other members. I do not know of any other meaning for the word 'advise' except 'advise.' The Council advises, and it can not advise without the vote of the United States. Why gentlemen should fear that the Congress of the United States would be advised to do something that it did not want to do I frankly can not imagine, because they can not even be advised to do anything unless their own representative has participated in the advice. It may be that that will impair somewhat the vigor of the League, but, nevertheless, the fact is so, that we are not obliged to take any advice except our own, which to any man who wants to go his own course is a very satisfactory state of affairs. Every man regards his own advice as best, and I dare say every man mixes his own advice with some thought of his own interest. Whether we use it wisely or unwisely, we can use the vote of the United States to make impossible drawing the United States into any enterprise that she does not care to be drawn into.

Yet article 10 strikes at the taproot of war. Article 10 is a statement that the very things that always have been sought in imperialistic wars are henceforth forgone by every ambitious nation in the world. I would have felt very lonely, my fellow countrymen, and I would have felt very much disturbed if, sitting at the peace table in Paris, I had supposed that I was expounding my own ideas. Whether you believe it or not, I know the relative size of my own ideas; I know how they stand related in bulk and proportion to the moral judgements of my fellow countrymen, and I proposed nothing whatever at the peace table at Paris that I had not sufficiently certain knowledge embodied the moral judgement of the citizens of the United States. I had gone over there with, so to say, explicit instructions. Don't you remember that we laid down fourteen points which should contain the principles of the settlement? They were not my points. In every one of them I was conscientiously trying to read the thought of the people of the United States, and after I uttered those points I had every assurance given me that could be given me that they did speak the moral judgement of the United States and not my single judgement. ...

We are not dealing with the kind of document which this is represented by some gentlemen to be; and inasmuch as we are dealing with a document simon-pure in respect of the very principles we have professed and lived up to, we have got to do one or other of two things – we have got to adapt it or reject it. There is no middle course. You can not go in on a special-privilege basis of your own. I take it that you are too proud to ask to be exempted from responsibilities which the other members of the League will carry. We go in upon equal terms or we do not go in at all; and if we do not go in, my fellow citizens, think of the tragedy of that result – the only sufficient guaranty to the peace of the world withheld! Ourselves drawn apart with that dangerous pride which means that we shall be ready to take care of ourselves, and that means we shall maintain great standing armies and an irresistible navy; that means we shall have the organization of a military nation; that means we shall have a general staff, with the kind of power that the general staff of Germany had, to mobilize this great manhood of the Nation when pleases, all the energy of our young men drawn into the thought and preparation for war. What of our pledges to the men that lie dead in France? We said that they went over there, not to prove the prowess of America or her readiness for another war but to see to it that there never was such a war again. It always seems to make it difficult for me to say anything, my fellow citizens, when I think of my clients in this case. My clients are the children; my clients are the next generation. They do not know what promises and bonds I undertook when I ordered the armies of the United States to the soil of France, but I know, and I intend to redeem my pledges to the children; they shall not be sent upon a similar errand. ...

My friends, on last Decoration Day I went to a beautiful hillside near Paris, where was located the cemetery of Suresnes, a cemetery given over to the burial of the American dead. Behind me on the slopes was rank upon rank of living American soldiers, and lying before me upon the levels of the plain was rank upon rank of departed American soldiers. Right by the side of the stand where I spoke there was a little group of French women who had adopted those graves, had made themselves mothers of those dear ghosts by putting flowers every day upon those graves, taking them as their own sons, their own beloved, because they had died in the same cause – France was free and the world was free because America had come! I wish some men in public life who are now opposing the settlement for which these men died could visit such a spot as that. I wish that the thought that comes out of those graves could penetrate their consciousness. I wish that they could feel the moral obligation that rests upon us not to go back on those boys, but to see the thing through, to see it through to the end and make good their redemption of the world. For nothing less depends upon this decision, nothing less than the liberation and salvation of the world.

A. Link (ed.), [8], pp. 500–13.

In Three Soldiers, *the renowned American writer and First World War veteran, John Dos Passos, presents a dismal portrait of the war experience. Rather than serving a glorious cause, soldiers find themselves helplessly trapped within a military machine where oppression, hate, boredom and vulgarity eventually destroy their souls. In this exchange, a wounded soldier confronts a 'Y' man, one of the volunteers the Young Men's Christian Association (YMCA) sent to France to organize wholesome recreational activities in the AEF and give spiritual counsel to soldiers.*

John Andrews awoke to feel a cold hand on his head.

'Feeling all right?' said a voice in his ear.

He found himself looking in a puffy, middle-aged face, with a lean nose and grey eyes, with dark rings under them. Andrews felt the eyes looking over him inquisitively. He saw the red triangle on the man's khaki sleeve.

'Yes,' he said.

'If you don't mind, I'd like to talk to you a little while, buddy.'

'Not a bit; have you got a chair?' said Andrews smiling.

'I don't suppose it was just right of me to wake you up, but you see it was this way. ... You were the next in line, an' I was afraid I'd forget you, if I skipped you.'

'I understand,' said Andrews, with a sudden determination to take the initiative away from the 'Y' man. 'How long have you been in France? D'you like the war?' he asked hurriedly.

The 'Y' man smiled sadly.

'You seem pretty spry,' he said. 'I guess you're in a hurry to get back at the front and get some more Huns.' He smiled again, with an air of indulgence.

Andrews did not answer.

'No, sonny, I don't like it here,' the 'Y' man said, after a pause. 'I wish I was home – but it's great to feel you're doing your duty.'

'It must be,' said Andrews.

'Have you heard about the great air raids our boys have pulled off? They've bombarded Frankfort; now if they could only wipe Berlin off the map.'

'Say, d'you hate 'em awful hard?' said Andrews in a low voice. 'Because if you do, I can tell you something will tickle you most to death. ... Lean over.'

The 'Y' man leant over curiously.

'Some German prisoners come to this hospital at six every night to get the garbage; now all you need to do if you really hate 'em so bad is borrow a revolver from one of your officer friends, and just shoot up the convoy. ...'

'Say ... where were you raised, boy?' The 'Y' man sat up suddenly with a look of alarm on his face. 'Don't you know that prisoners are sacred?'

'D'you know what our colonel told us before going into the Argonne offensive? The more prisoners we took, the less grub there'ld be; and do you know what happened to the prisoners that were taken? Why do you hate the Huns?'

'Because they are barbarians, enemies of civilization. You must have enough education to know that,' said the 'Y' man, raising his voice angrily. 'What church do you belong to?'

'None.'

'But you must have been connected with some church, boy. You can't have been raised a heathen in America. Every Christian belongs or has belonged to some church or other from baptism.'

'I make no pretensions to Christianity.'

Andrews closed his eyes and turned his head away. He could feel the 'Y' man hovering over him irresolutely. After a while he opened his eyes. The 'Y' man was leaning over the next bed. ...

As soon as he got out of the hospital he would desert; the determination formed suddenly in his mind, making the excited blood surge gloriously through his body. There was nothing else to do; he would desert. He pictured himself hobbling away in the dark on his lame legs, stripping his uniform off, losing himself in some out of the way corner of France, or slipping by the sentries to Spain and freedom. He was ready to endure anything, to face any sort of death, for the sake of a few months of liberty in which to forget the degradation of this last year. This was his last run with the pack.

J. Dos Passos, [40], pp. 209–10.

CHRONOLOGY

1914

28 June	Archduke Franz Ferdinand assassinated by Gavrilo Princip in Sarajevo, Bosnia.
23 July	Austria-Hungary presents Serbia with ultimatum.
25 July	Serbia mobilizes after accepting all but one Austro-Hungarian condition.
28 July	Austria-Hungary declares war on Serbia.
29 July	Austria-Hungary invades Serbia.
30 July	Russia orders general mobilization of military forces.
1 August	Germany declares war on Russia.
2 August	German troops enter Luxembourg.
3 August	German troops enter Belgium, Germany declares war on France.
4 August	Great Britain declares war on Germany, President Woodrow Wilson announces US neutrality.
6 August	Austria-Hungary declares war on Russia.
23 August	Japan declares war on Germany.
24 August	German army enters France.
5–10 September	First Battle of the Marne – Paris saved from invading German army.
1 November	Russia declares war on Ottoman Empire.
29 December	Wilson protests British search of US ships for contraband.

1915

30 January	Wilson sends advisor, Colonel Edward House, on first peace mission to Europe.
4 February	Germany declares waters around Britain a war zone.
10 February	American government vows to hold Germans strictly accountable for U-boat sinkings of US ships.
11 March	Britain announces blockade of German ports.
30 March	Wilson protests British blockade.
7 May	German submarine sinks the *Lusitania* off the coast of Ireland.
23 May	Italy declares war on Austria-Hungary.

7 June	Bryan resigns as Secretary of State in protest over Wilson's response to the *Lusitania* crisis.
9 June	Wilson protests German policy of unconditional submarine warfare.
21 July	Wilson sends a third note to Germany demanding that they respect US rights as neutrals.
19 August	German submarine sinks British passenger ship, the *Arabic*.
26 August	Italy declares war on Germany.
1 September	Germany issues *Arabic* Pledge agreeing to warn passenger ships of U-boat attack.

1916

22 February	Wilson sends advisor House on second peace mission to Europe.
9 March	Francisco 'Pancho' Villa attacks Columbus, New Mexico, with 1,500 troops and kills seventeen Americans.
15 March	Pershing enters Mexico with 6,000 troops in pursuit of Pancho Villa.
24 March	German U-boat sinks the *Sussex*, an unarmed French channel ship.
18 April	Wilson warns Germany to end sinkings or the United States will sever diplomatic relations.
4 May	German government issues the *Sussex* Pledge, refraining from attacks on merchant or passenger ships except in self-defense.
3 June	National Defense Act increases the size of the regular army and National Guard.
21 June	Mexican and American troops clash in Carrizal, Mexico.
18 July	British government blacklists eighty American firms for trading with Germany.
28 July	The United States and Mexico agree to mediation.
7 November	Wilson re-elected President, defeating Charles Evans Hughes by 277–254 electoral votes.

1917

16 January	German Foreign Minister, Alfred Zimmerman, sends telegram to Mexico to solicit its help in a war against the United States. It is intercepted by British intelligence.
22 January	Wilson delivers 'peace without victory' speech.
1 February	Germany resumes unconditional submarine warfare.
3 February	United States breaks off diplomatic relations with Germany.

1 March	Contents of Zimmerman telegram made public.
12 March	Wilson orders merchant ships armed.
15 March	Tsar Nicholas II abdicates his throne in Russia.
6 April	The United States declares war on Germany.
14 April	Committee on Public Information created to control flow of wartime information.
30 April	Allies begin convoy system to combat submarine warfare.
10 May	Pershing appointed commander of American Expeditionary Forces.
18 May	Wilson signs Selective Service Act authorizing wartime conscription.
26 May	First American troops arrive in France.
5 June	First national draft registration day draws 10 million men to 4,000 draft centers.
15 June	Congress passes Espionage Act.
10 August	Congress passes Lever Food and Fuel Act to conserve resources.
21 October	First American troops enter the line in Lunéville, France.
24 October–10 November	Italians routed in battle of Caporetto.
7 November	Bolsheviks overthrow Russian Provisional Government and assume power.
3 December	Bolshevik Russian government signs armistice with Germany.
7 December	The United States declares war on Austria-Hungary.
18 December	Eighteenth Amendment on prohibition sent to states for ratification.
26 December	US government takes over railways for duration of war.

1918

8 January	Wilson gives Fourteen Points Speech.
3 March	Treaty of Brest-Litovsk ends war between Russia and Germany.
21 March–17 July	German spring offensives on the western front.
26 March	Foch made supreme commander of Allied armies on the western front.
16 May	Congress passes Sedition Act.
25 May	German U-boats enter American waters.
27 May–5 June	Battle of Chateau-Thierry
28–31 May	First offensive American action in the Battle of Cantigny.
6–25 June	Battle of Belleau Wood.

6 July	Wilson agrees to send troops to Siberia.
18 July–6 August	Americans fight in Allied Aisne–Marne counter-offensive.
16 August	American troops arrive in Vladivostok, East Siberia.
18 August– 12 October	Americans fight in Allied Oise–Aisne offensive.
4 September	American troops arrive in Archangel, North Russia.
12–16 September	St Mihiel Offensive.
14 September	Socialist leader, Eugene V. Debs, sentenced to ten years in prison for violating Espionage Act.
26 September– 11 November	Meuse–Argonne campaign.
3–4 October	Germany proposes peace based on the Fourteen Points.
5 November	Republicans gain control of Congress in mid-term elections.
9 November	Wilhelm II abdicates and goes to Holland, Germany becomes a republic.
11 November	Armistice between Allies and Germany.

1919

18 January	Peace negotiations begin in Paris.
29 January	Eighteenth Amendment, enacting prohibition, ratified.
15 March	American Legion founded in Paris.
3 June	American troops begin leaving North Russia.
28 June	Germany signs the Versailles Treaty.
5 August	American headquarters closed in North Russia.
1 September	Last American combat division leaves France.
26 September	Wilson suffers a stroke while on speaking tour in favor of Versailles Treaty.
19 November	Senate rejects the Versailles Treaty for first time.

1920

3 January	Last American troops leave France.
26 January	American troops begin leaving Siberia, Russia.
19 March	Senate rejects Versailles Treaty with and without Lodge reservations.
1 April	Last American troops withdrawn from Siberia, Russia.
26 August	Nineteenth Amendment, granting female suffrage, ratified.
2 November	Warren G. Harding elected President of the United States.

1921

19 May   First of many restrictive immigration acts establishing quotas signed by Harding.

2 July   Harding signs Congressional joint resolution ending war with Germany.

25 August   Peace treaty between the United States and Germany signed.

1923

24 January   Last American troops leave Germany.

1924

18 March   Adjusted Compensation certificates issued to American veterans.

24 May   National Origins Act limits immigration to 150,000 and establishes national quotas.

1932

29 May–28 July   Bonus March on Washington, DC.

8 November   Franklin D. Roosevelt defeats Herbert Hoover in presidential election.

1936

29 February   Congress overrides presidential veto to pay veterans their bonus.

GLOSSARY

Allies The term used to refer to the countries (Belgium, the British Empire, China, France, Italy, Japan, Russia, and Serbia) at war with the Central Powers. The US joined the Allied side as an Associated Power to protect its independence.

American Expeditionary Force (AEF) The name given to the American military forces serving along the western front. By November 1918 the AEF numbered 2 million troops, including 1.3 million combatant troops. During the war 50,280 American soldiers died in combat.

American Legion The American World War I veterans' organization founded in March 1919 in Paris by Theodore Roosevelt, Jr. and other prominent advocates of military preparedness. Eschewing party politics, the Legion focused on combating radicalism, securing adjusted compensation and medical benefits for veterans, and drafted the GI Bill of Rights in 1944.

Armistice The negotiated suspension of hostilities that occurred on the eastern and western fronts before peace negotiations. The Allied cease-fire with Germany began at 11:00 a.m. on 11 November 1918. The armistice agreement required Germany to evacuate its army from occupied territory within fourteen days, to surrender a significant portion of its military materials, to annul its peace treaty with Russia, and gave the Allies the right to occupy the Rhineland. The Allied blockade remained in effect, and the Allies reserved the right to resume hostilities within forty-eight hours if Germany deviated from these terms.

Blockade Both sides used their naval forces to disrupt the enemy's trade during the First World War. The British relied on their superior navy to halt food and munitions imports to the Central Powers while Germany used its new fleet of U-boats to interrupt trade between the United States and the Allies. Debates over whether each side pursued their economic warfare in a manner consistent with international law influenced the American decision to enter the war.

Bolshevik The name used to describe one who believes in a classless society which comes about through revolution. The Bolsheviks seized power in Russia on 7 November 1917. American fears of a bolshevik revolution spreading to the United States led to the 'Red Scare' in 1919.

Bonus March Protest in 1932 by 40,000 veterans who camped in Washington, DC for two months to demand the immediate payment of their adjusted compensation certificates. General Douglas MacArthur used troops to evict the veterans, and this clash became a *cause célèbre* that illustrated to many Americans President Herbert Hoover's inability to comprehend the extent of Depression-induced suffering in the United States.

Central Powers Term used to describe the countries (the German, Austro-Hungarian, and Ottoman Empires, and Bulgaria) at war with the Allies.

Convoy The system adopted in 1917 by the Allies which used battleships to protect groups of merchant ships from German U-boat attacks as they traversed the Atlantic. British and American anti-submarine craft accompanied convoys, and by late 1918 had driven German U-boats from the seas.

Fourteen Points A program for peace announced by President Wilson in a speech to Congress on 8 January 1918. The proposal called for the renunciation of secret treaties, the freedom of the seas, open trade, arms reductions, self-determination, an international organization dedicated to collective security, and outlined specific solutions to territorial disputes in Europe.

Hindenburg Line A fortified line along the western front that the Germans began constructing in 1916. The defensive system consisted of fortified strongholds with trenches, artillery, and barbed wire. In 1918, the Allies faced the significant challenge of breaking through this line of fortifications.

League of Nations The collective security organization, first proposed in the Fourteen Points, that Wilson successfully incorporated into the 1919 Paris Peace Settlement. Opposition from Republican Senators to the League as an infringement on American sovereignty caused the Senate to reject the Versailles Treaty. The United States, consequently, never joined the League of Nations.

Lusitania The British passenger liner, transporting munitions and passengers, that was sunk by a German U-boat on 7 May 1915 off the coast of Ireland. The attack killed 1,198 people, including 128 Americans. An outraged President Wilson demanded, and eventually received, an apology from Germany. Germany soon suspended surprise attacks on passenger ships to appease mounting American anger in response to the subsequent sinking of the *Arabic*, an empty British passenger ship, on 19 August 1915.

Mandate Territory given in trust to a League of Nation member nation to govern. As part of the Paris Peace Settlement, former German colonies in Africa and Ottoman territories in the Middle East were distributed to victorious European nations. In theory, the trustees were charged with preparing these lands for independence. In reality, mandates were incorporated into existing colonial empires.

Meuse–Argonne campaign A forty-seven-day battle fought in the American sector of the western front between the Argonne Forest and the Meuse River which began on 26 September 1918 and lasted until the Armistice. Nearly 1.2 million American soldiers participated, the largest American military effort to date. As part of the general Allied thrust along all parts of the western front in the fall of 1918, the Meuse–Argonne campaign contributed significantly to the final Allied victory.

New Deal A blanket term used to describe President Franklin D. Roosevelt's wide-ranging legislative programs in the 1930s to end suffering and reform American society during the Great Depression. The New Deal provided direct economic and work relief to American citizens, regulated the nation's financial institutions, and established landmark reforms such as an old-age pension system and fair labor standards.

Schlieffen Plan The war plan created in 1905 by the German Chief of Staff, Alfred von Schlieffen, to avert the problem of a two-front war in the advent of Germany going to war with the allied nations of France and Russia. The plan called for

Germany to take the advantage of a slowly mobilizing Russian army to defeat France quickly by invading from the north through Belgium, then turning its full army against Russia. A modified version of the Schlieffen Plan failed in August 1914 when human endurance, logistical difficulties, and communication problems hampered the German army's drive to Paris. The result was the entry of Britain into the war in response to the violation of Belgian neutrality, and trench stalemate.

Versailles Peace Treaty The peace treaty that ended the war between the Allies and Germany. The massive treaty contained numerous controversial clauses, including ones regarding German war guilt, German reparation payments to the Allies, the League of Nations, the mandate system, and a re-drawn map of eastern Europe along ethnic lines. Under protest, Germany signed the treaty on 28 June 1919. The US Senate rejected it twice and in 1921 concluded an independent peace treaty with Germany.

Zimmerman telegram The telegram sent on 16 January 1917 by German foreign minister, Arthur Zimmerman, instructing the German ambassador to Mexico to offer the Mexicans help in recovering Texas, New Mexico, and Arizona (territories lost in the Mexican–American War of 1846–48) if they started a borderland war with the United States and asked Japan to join them. British intelligence agents intercepted the telegram and gave it to the State Department. Its publication two months later hardened American opinion against Germany.

Baker, Newton (1871–1937) American Secretary of War, 1916–21. A reforming Democratic mayor of Cleveland, and a known pacifist, Baker oversaw implementation of the nation's massive conscription effort. Baker supported Pershing's desire to create an independent army. Though he privately disagreed with Wilson's decision to send American troops to Russia, Baker loyally served Wilson and enjoyed the President's complete confidence.

Bryan, William Jennings (1860–1925) American Secretary of State, 1913–15. Bryan ran unsuccessfully for President three times before the First World War. He resigned as Secretary of State in 1915 to protest Wilson's strongly-worded demands to Germany in the wake of the sinking of the *Lusitania*, which he believed would lead to war.

Clemenceau, Georges (1841–1929) Prime Minister and War Minister of France, 1917–20. Nicknamed the 'Tiger', Clemenceau began the war as a strong critic of the French government's censorship policies and of pacifists. He ended it as Prime Minister and Wilson's chief rival at the Paris Peace Conference, where the two clashed over how to punish Germany, protect France's borders, and ensure world peace.

Creel, George (1876–1953) A leading muckraker journalist who became head of the Committee on Public Information (CPI), the agency charged with disseminating official information and propaganda. The CPI used printed media (in numerous foreign languages), movies, photos, posters and speakers (the famous Four-Minute Men) to foster public support for the war.

Foch, Marshall Ferdinand (1851–1928) A tireless advocate of an offensive military strategy, Foch helped save Paris during the First Battle of the Marne in 1914, commanded French forces during the Battle of the Somme in 1916, and became Supreme Commander of the Allied armies on the western front in 1918. Taking advantage of German exhaustion in the wake of their failed spring offensives, Foch master-minded the massive Allied fall offensive that won the war for the Allies.

Franz Ferdinand, Archduke (1863–1914) Heir to the Austro-Hungarian throne whose assassination by Gavrilo Princip, a member of a radical Serbian nationalist group, during a trip to Sarajevo, Bosnia, on 28 June 1914 set off the chain of events leading to world war. Franz Ferdinand wanted to use his trip to improve relations between the monarchy and the recently annexed province, which Austria-Hungary received from the Ottoman Empire in 1908. Instead, his visit on a Serbian national holiday antagonized those Bosnian Serbs yearning to unite with independent Serbia.

Hindenburg, Field Marshall Paul von (1847–1934) Commander-in-Chief of the German army, 1916–18 who launched the massive spring offensive in 1918, hoping to end the war before the Americans arrived. The assault failed, exhausting the Germany army and preparing the way to the successful Allied counter-offensive that won the war.

Hoover, Herbert (1874–1964)   As director of the Food Administration (1917–18) and coordinator of massive food relief programs to starving European refugees during and after the war, Hoover developed a worldwide reputation for his humanitarian endeavors. Hoover served as President of the United States, 1928–32. In marked contrast to his earlier image, Hoover's popularity plummeted because he appeared indifferent to the plight of the common man during the new Depression crisis.

Lansing, Robert (1864–1928)   He became Secretary of State in 1915 after Bryan resigned, and served in this position until 1920. Lansing viewed Germany as a threat to western civilization, and was a key advisor urging Wilson to respond forcefully to German violations of American neutrality rights. Lansing had less faith in the principal of self-determination and the League of Nations than Wilson, emphasizing instead the importance of spreading democracy. Due to his differences with the President, Lansing played a minimal role in the Versailles Peace Conference.

Lenin, Vladimir (1870–1924)   The Bolshevik revolutionary who returned, with German help, from exile in Switzerland and seized control of Russia in November 1917. Lenin signed a separate peace with Germany, then struggled against counter-revolutionary armies and Allied Interventions to retain his power.

Lodge, Henry Cabot (1850–1924)   Republican Senator from Massachusetts, Senate Majority Leader and Chairman of Senate Foreign Affairs Committee, who led the fight to defeat ratification of the Versailles Treaty by the United States. Lodge believed an alliance between the United States and the European victors would ensure world peace and serve American national interests better than the League of Nations. Lodge authored reservations to the treaty to clarify American obligations to the League of Nations which Wilson refused to accept. In the wake of the treaty fight, the country rejected both Wilson's idea of collective security and Lodge's notion of balance-of-power internationalism in favor of insular nationalism.

Pershing, John Joseph (1860–1948)   He served as Commander-in-Chief of the American Expeditionary Force, 1917–18. Dedicated to a strategy of open warfare, Pershing had complete authority to create and command an independent American army along the western front. On 5 September 1919 Pershing became the second general, after George Washington, to hold the rank of General of the Armies.

Pétain, Marshal Philippe (1856–1951)   A hero of the French defense of Verdun in 1916, Pétain succeeded disgraced General Robert Nivelle as Commander-in-Chief of the French army in 1917 and quelled the mutinies sweeping through the French army in the wake of Nivelle's failed Chemin des Dames offensive. Pétain unsuccessfully lobbied Pershing to amalgamate American troops into French units.

Wilhelm II (1859–1941)   The last emperor of Germany (1888–1918) who believed Germany's status as a world power depended on its military achievements. The Kaiser selected the men who commanded the Germany army, and made the critical decisions regarding submarine warfare. He abdicated and fled to Holland when President Wilson made his removal a condition for peace.

Wilson, Woodrow (1856–1924) President of the United States, 1912–20. He kept the United States out of the war for two and a half years before leading the country on a crusade to fight 'the war to end all wars.' The principles Wilson articulated throughout his Presidency shaped American foreign policy throughout the twentieth century.

BIBLIOGRAPHY

The place of publication is New York unless otherwise stated.

PRIMARY SOURCES

1 Aptheker, H. (ed.), *A Documentary History of the Negro People in the United States, 1910–1932*, Citadel Press, 1990.
2 Ayres, L., *The War with Germany: A Statistical Summary*, Government Printing Office, Washington, DC, 1919.
3 Bourne, R., *The Radical Will: Selected Writings, 1911–1918*, University of California Press, Berkeley, CA, 1992.
4 Bullard, R. L., *American Soldiers Also Fought*, Longmans, Green & Co., 1936.
5 Chambers, III, J. W. (ed.), *The Eagle and the Dove: The American Peace Movement and U.S. Foreign Policy, 1900–1922*, 2nd edn, Syracuse University Press, Syracuse, NY, 1991.
6 Debs, Eugene V., *Writings and Speeches of Eugene V. Debs*, Hermitage Press, 1948.
7 Dudley, W. (ed.), *World War I: Opposing Viewpoints*, Greenhaven Press, San Diego, CA, 1998.
8 Link, A. (ed.), *The Papers of Woodrow Wilson*, 69 vols, Princeton University Press, Princeton, NJ, 1986.
9 Ludendorff, E., *Ludendorff's Own Story: August 1914–November 1918*, vol. 2, Harper & Brothers, 1919.
10 McAdoo, W. G., *Crowded Years*, Kennikat Press, Port Washington, NY, 1971.
11 *The New York Times*, 18 June 1932.
12 Trask, D. (ed.), *World War I at Home: Readings on American Life, 1914–1920*, Wiley, 1970.
13 *The Treaties of Peace, 1919–1923*, vol. 1, Carnegie Endowment for International Peace, 1924.

SECONDARY SOURCES

African-Americans

14 Barbeau, Arthur and Florette, Henri, *The Unknown Soldiers: Black American Troops in World War I*, Temple University Press, Philadelphia, PA, 1974.
15 Du Bois, W. E. B., *Darkwater*, in E. J. Sundquist (ed.), *The Oxford W. E. B. Du Bois Reader*, Oxford University Press, 1996.
16 Ellis, M., "'Close ranks" and "seeking honors": W. E. B. Du Bois in World War I', *Journal of American History*, 79, June 1992, pp. 96–124.

17 Gottlieb, P., *Making Their Own Way: Southern Blacks' Migration to Pittsburgh, 1916–30*, University of Illinois Press, Urbana, IL, 1997.

18 Grossman, J. R., *Land of Hope: Chicago, Black Southerners and the Great Migration*, University of Chicago Press, Chicago, IL, 1989.

19 Haynes, R.V., *A Night of Violence: The Houston Riot of 1917*, Louisiana State University Press, Baton Rouge, LA, 1976.

20 Jordan, W., "'The damnable dilemma": African-American accommodation and protest during World War I', *The Journal of American History*, 81, 1995, pp. 1562–90.

21 Lewis, D.L., *W.E.B. Du Bois: Biography of a Race, 1868–1919*, Henry Holt, 1993.

22 Lewis, D. L., *When Harlem Was in Vogue*, Penguin Books, 1997.

23 Nalty, B. C., *Strength for the Fight – A History of Black Americans in the Military*, The Free Press, 1986.

24 Rudwick, E. M., *Race Riot at East St. Louis, 2 July 1917*, University of Illinois Press, Urbana, IL, 1982.

25 Tuttle, Jr., W. M., *Race Riot: Chicago in the Red Summer of 1919*, Atheneum, 1970.

American Intervention in Mexico and Russia

26 Foglesong, D. S., *America's Secret War against Bolshevism*, University of North Carolina Press, Chapel Hill, NC, 1995.

27 Gardner, L. C., *Safe for Democracy: The Anglo-American Response to Revolution, 1913–23*, Oxford University Press, 1984.

28 Katz, F., *The Secret War in Mexico: Europe, the United States and the Mexican Revolution*, University of Chicago Press, Chicago, IL, 1981.

29 Kennan, G. F., *Soviet–American Relations, 1917–1920*, 2 vols, Princeton University Press, Princeton, NJ, 1956.

30 Levin, N. G., *Woodrow Wilson and World Politics: America's Response to War and Revolution*, Oxford University Press, 1968.

31 Long, J. W., 'American intervention in Russia: the North Russian Expedition, 1918–19', *Diplomatic History*, 6, 1982, pp. 45–67.

32 Maddox, R. J., *The Unknown War with Russia: Wilson's Siberian Intervention*, Presidio Press, San Rafael, CA, 1977.

33 McFadden, D. W., *Alternative Paths: Soviets and Americans, 1917–1920*, Oxford University Press, 1993.

34 Rhodes, B. D., *The Anglo-American Winter War with Russia, 1918–1919*, Greenwood Press, Westport, CT, 1988.

35 Schmitt, K., *Mexico and the United States, 1821–1973: Conflict and Coexistence*, Wiley, 1974.

36 Trani, E. P., 'Woodrow Wilson and the decision to intervene in Russia: a reconsideration', *Journal of Modern History*, 48, 1976, pp. 440–61.

37 Unterberger, B. M., *America's Siberian Adventure, 1918–1920: A Study of National Policy*, Duke University Press, Durham, NC, 1956.

38 Williams, W. A., 'American intervention in Russia, 1917–1920', *Studies on the Left*, 3, 1963, pp. 24–48.

Fiction

39 cummings, e. e., *The Enormous Room*, Modern Library, 1934.
40 Dos Passos, J., *Three Soldiers*, Houghton Mifflin Co., Boston, MA, 1949.
41 Dos Passos, J., *USA*, Library of America, 1996.
42 Hemingway, E., *A Farewell to Arms*, Scribner's, 1929.
43 March, W., *Company K*, University of Alabama Press, Tuscaloosa, AL, 1989.

Film

44 'All Quiet on the Western Front' (1930), dir. Lewis Milestone.
45 'Gallipoli' (1982), dir. Peter Weir.
46 'The Grand Illusion' (1937), dir. Jean Renoir.
47 'The Great War and the Shaping of the 20th Century' (1996, documentary), dir. Blaine Baggett.
48 'Life and Nothing But' (1990), dir. Bertrand Taverneir.
49 'Oh! What a Lovely War' (1969), dir. Richard Attenborough.
50 'Paths of Glory' (1957), dir. Stanley Kubrick.
51 'Sergeant York' (1941), dir. Howard Hawks.

General Histories and Reference Works

52 American Battle Monuments Commission, *American Armies and Battlefields in Europe: A History, Guide, and Reference Book*, Center for Military History, Washington, DC, 1992.
53 Carnes, M., Garraty, J. and Williams, P. (eds), *Mapping America's Past: A Historical Atlas*, Henry Holt, 1996.
54 Cooper, J. M. and Neu, C. E. (eds), *The Wilson Era*, Harlan Davidson, Arlington Heights, IL, 1991.
55 Gilbert, M., *The First World War: A Complete History*, Henry Holt and Co., 1994.
56 Gray, R., *Chronicle of the First World War*, 2 vols, Facts on File, 1990.
57 Link, A., *The Impact of World War I*, Harper & Row, 1969.
58 Merriman, J., *A History of Modern Europe: From the Renaissance to the Present*, W. W. Norton & Co., 1996.
59 Smith, P., *America Enters the World*, Viking Penguin, 1991.
60 Stokesbury, J. L., *A Short History of World War I*, Morrow, 1981.
61 Tansil, C. C., *America Goes to War*, Little, Brown & Co., Boston, MA, 1938.
62 Venzon, A. C., *The United States in the First World War: An Encyclopedia*, Garland Publishing, 1995.
63 Winter, J. M., *The Experience of World War I*, Oxford University Press, 1995.

Homefront: Economic Mobilization

64 Breen, W. J., *Uncle Sam at Home: Civilian Mobilization, Wartime Federalism, and the Council of National Defense, 1917–1919*, Greenwood Press, Westport, CT, 1984.

65 Clark, J. M., *The Cost of the World War to the American People*, Yale University Press, New Haven, CT, 1931.

66 Conner, V., *The National War Labor Board: Stability, Social Justice, and the Voluntary State in World War I*, University of North Carolina Press, Chapel Hill, NC, 1983.

67 Cuff, R. D., *The War Industries Board*, Johns Hopkins University Press, Baltimore, MD, 1973.

68 Dubofsky, M., *We Shall Be All: A History of the Industrial Workers of the World*, Quadrangle Books, Chicago, IL, 1969.

69 Gilbert, C., *American Financing of World War I*, Greenwood, Westport, CT, 1970.

70 Godfrey, A. A., *Government Operation of the Railroads: Its Necessity, Success, and Consequences, 1918–1920*, Jenkins Publishing Co., Austin, TX, 1974.

71 Grubbs, F. L., *The Struggle for Labor Loyalty, Gompers, the A.F. of L. and the Pacifists, 1917–1920*, Duke University Press, Durham, NC, 1968.

72 Grubbs, F. L., *Samuel Gompers and the Great War: Protecting Labors' Standards*, Meridional Publications, Wake Forest, NC, 1982.

73 Grundstein, N., *Presidential Delegation of Authority in Wartime*, University of Pittsburgh Press, Pittsburgh, PA, 1961.

74 Hawley, E., *The Great War and the Search for a Modern Order: A History of the American People and their Institutions, 1917–1933*, St Martin's Press, 1979.

75 Kennedy, D., *Over Here: The First World War and American Society*, Oxford University Press, 1980.

76 Kerr, K. A., *American Railroad Politics, 1914–1920; Rates, Wages, and Efficiency*, University of Pittsburgh Press, Pittsburgh, PA, 1969.

77 Koistinen, P. A. C., *The Military–Industrial Complex: A Historical Perspective*, Praeger, 1980.

78 Koistinen, P. A. C., *Mobilizing for Modern War: The Political Economy of American Warfare, 1865–1919*, University of Kansas Press, Lawrence, KS, 1997.

79 Leuchtenburg, W. E., 'The New Deal and the analogue of war' in J. Braemen (ed.), *Change and Continuity in Twentieth Century America*, Ohio State University Press, Columbus, OH, 1965.

80 Nash, G. D., *U.S. Oil Policy, 1890–1964*, University of Pittsburgh Press, Pittsburgh, PA, 1968.

81 Paul, R., *Taxation for Prosperity*, Bobbs-Merrill, Indianapolis, IN, 1947.

82 Schaffer, R., *America in the Great War: The Rise of the War Welfare State*, Oxford University Press, 1991.

83 Sklar, M., *The Corporate Reconstruction of American Capitalism, 1890–1916: The Market, the Law and Politics*, Cambridge University Press, 1988.

Lost Generation, the Bonus March and the GI Bill

84 Bennett, M. J., *When Dreams Came True: The GI Bill and the Making of Modern America*, Brassey's, Washington, DC, 1996.

85 Bernstein, I., 'The bonus army', in T. R. Frazier and J. M. Blum (eds), *The Underside of American History*, vol. 2, Harcourt Brace Jovanovich, Inc., 1974.

86 Cohen, W. I., *The American Revisionists: The Lessons of Intervention in World War I*, University of Chicago Press, Chicago, IL, 1967.

87 Cooperman, S., *World War I and the American Novel*, Johns Hopkins University Press, Baltimore, MD, 1967.

88 Daniels, R., *The Bonus March: An Episode of the Great Depression*, Greenwood Press, Westport, CT, 1971.

89 Lisio, D. J., *The President and Protest: Hoover, Conspiracy, and the Bonus Riot*, University Missouri Press, Columbia, MO, 1974.

90 Lisio, D. J., 'United States: bread and butter politics', in Stephen Ward (ed.), *The War Generation: Veterans of the First World War*, Kennikat Press, Port Washington, NY, 1975.

91 Pencak, W., *For God and Country: The American Legion, 1919–1941*, Northeastern University Press, Boston, MA, 1989.

92 Piehler, G. K., *Remembering War the American Way*, Smithsonian Institution Press, Washington, DC, 1995.

93 Ross, D., *Preparing for Ulysses: Politics and Veterans during World War II*, Columbia University Press, 1969.

94 Severo, R. and Milford, L., *The Wages of War: When American Soldiers Come Home – From Valley Forge to Vietnam*, Simon and Schuster, 1989.

The Military Experience

95 Barsh, R. L., 'American Indians in the Great War', *Ethnohistory*, 38, 1991, pp. 276–303.

96 Braim, P. F., *The Test of Battle: The American Expeditionary Forces in the Meuse–Argonne Campaign*, University of Delaware Press, Newark, DE, 1987.

97 Chambers, III, J. W., *To Raise An Army: The Draft Comes to Modern America*, The Free Press, 1987.

98 Coffman, E., *The War to End All Wars: The American Military Experience in World War*, Oxford University Press, 1968.

99 Crosby, Jr., A., *Epidemic and Peace, 1918*, Greenwood Press, Westport, CT, 1976.

100 Ford, N. G., '"Mindful of the traditions of his race": dual identity and foreign-born soldiers in the First World War American army', *Journal of American Ethnic History*, 16, 1997, pp. 35–57.

101 Gould, S. J., *The Mismeasure of Man*, W. W. Norton, 1981.

102 James, D. C., *The Years of MacArthur, 1880–1941*, vol. 1, Houghton Mifflin Co., Boston, MA, 1970.

103 Keene, J. D., 'Intelligence and morale in the army of a democracy: the genesis of military psychology during the First World War', *Military Psychology*, 6, 1994, pp. 235–53.

104 Keene, J. D., 'Uneasy alliances: French military intelligence and the American army during the First World War', *Intelligence and National Security*, 13, 1998, pp. 18–36.

105 Kevles, D. J., 'Testing the army's intelligence: psychologists and the military in World War I', *Journal of American History*, 55, 1968, pp. 565–81.

106 Langer, W. L., *Gas and Flame in World War I*, Knopf, 1965.

107 Lee, D. D., *Sergeant York: An American Hero*, University Press of Kentucky, Lexington, KY, 1985.

108 Meigs, M., *Optimism at Armageddon: Voices of American Participants in the First World War*, New York University Press, 1997.

109 Millett, A. R., 'Cantigny, 28–31 May 1918', in C. E. Heller and W. A. Stofft (eds), *America's First Battles: 1776–1965*, University Press of Kansas, Lawrence, KS, 1986.

110 Millett, A. R., 'Over where? The AEF and the American strategy for victory, 1917–1918', in K. J. Hagan and W. R. Roberts (eds), *Against All Enemies: Interpretations of American Military History from Colonial Times to the Present*, Greenwood Press, Westport, CT, 1986.

111 Millett, A. R. and Maslowski, P., *For the Common Defense: A Military History of the United States of America*, The Free Press, 1984.

112 Millis, W., *Arms and Men: A Study in American Military History*, G. P. Putnam, 1956.

113 Nenninger, T. K., 'American military effectiveness during the First World War', in A. R. Millett and W. Murray (eds), *Military Effectiveness, Vol. 1: The First World War*, Allen & Unwin, Boston, MA, 1988.

114 Strecker, E. A., 'Military psychiatry: World War I, 1917–18', in American Psychiatric Association, *One Hundred Years of American Psychiatry*, Columbia University Press, 1944.

115 Trask, D. F., *The AEF and Coalition Warmaking, 1917–1918*, University Press of Kansas, Lawrence, KS, 1993.

116 Weigley, R. F., *History of the United States Army*, Macmillan Co., 1967.

117 White, B. W., 'The American Indian as a soldier, 1890–1919', *Canadian Review of American Studies*, 7, 1976, pp. 15–25.

118 White, B. W., 'The American military and the melting pot in World War I', in P. Karsten (ed.), *The Military in America*, The Free Press, 1980.

Origins of the War

119 Berghahn, V. R., *Germany and the Approach of War in 1914*, Macmillan, London, 1973.

120 Devlin, P., *Too Proud to Fight: Woodrow Wilson's Neutrality*, Oxford University Press, London, 1974.

121 DeWeerd, H. A., *President Wilson Fights His War: World War I and the American Intervention*, Macmillan, 1958.

122 Eksteins, M., *Rites of Spring: The Great War and the Birth of the Modern Age*, Houghton Mifflin, Boston, MA, 1989.

123 Fischer, F., *Germany's Aims in the First World War*, W. W. Norton, 1967.

124 Gregory, R., *The Origins of American Intervention in the First World War*, W. W. Norton, 1971.

125 Hatton, P. H. S., 'The First World War: Britain and Germany in 1914, the July crisis and war aims', *Past & Present*, 36, 1967, pp. 138–43.

126 Jonas, M., *The United States and Germany*, Cornell University Press, Ithaca, NY, 1984.

127 Koch, H. W. (ed.), *The Origins of the First World War: Great Power Rivalry and War Aims*, Taplinger, 1972.

128   Martel, G., *The Origins of the First World War*, Addison-Wesley, 1996.
129   May, E., *The World War and American Isolation, 1914–1917*, Harvard University Press, Cambridge, MA, 1959.
130   Miller, S. E., Lynn-Jones, S. M. and Van Evera, S. (eds), *Military Strategy and the Origins of the First World War*, Princeton University Press, Princeton, NJ, 1991.
131   Simpson, C., *The Lusitania*, Little, Brown, Boston, MA, 1972.
132   Smith, D. M., *Robert Lansing and American Neutrality, 1914–1917*, University of California Press, Berkeley, CA, 1958.
133   Stern, F., 'German historians and the war: Fritz Fischer and his critics', in F. Stern (ed.), *The Failure of Illiberalism: Essays on the Political Culture of Modern Germany*, Knopf, 1972.
134   Tuchman, B. W., *The Zimmerman Telegram*, Viking Press, 1958.

Paris Peace Conference

135   Ambrosius, L., *Woodrow Wilson and the American Diplomatic Tradition: The Treaty Fight in Perspective*, Cambridge University Press, 1987.
136   Ambrosius, L., *Wilsonian Statecraft*, Scholarly Resource Books, Wilmington, DE, 1991.
137   Baily, T. A., *Woodrow Wilson and the Lost Peace*, Macmillan, 1944.
138   Keynes, J. M., *The Economic Consequences of the Peace*, Harcourt, Brace, and Howe, 1920.
139   Knock, T. J., *To End All Wars: Woodrow Wilson and the Quest for a New World Order*, Oxford University Press, 1992.
140   Lauren, P. G., 'Human rights in history: diplomacy and racial equality at the Paris peace conference', *Diplomatic History*, 2, 1978, pp. 257–78.
141   Levin, N. G., *Woodrow Wilson and World Politics: America's Response to War and Revolution*, Oxford University Press, 1968.
142   Link, A. S., 'The higher realism of Woodrow Wilson', *Journal of Presbyterian History*, 41, 1963, pp. 1–13.
143   Marks, S., 'The myths of reparations', *Central European History*, 18, 1978, pp. 231–55.
144   Mayer, A. J., *The Political Origins of the New Diplomacy, 1917–1918*, Yale University Press, New Haven, CT, 1959.
145   Mayer, A. J., *The Politics and Diplomacy of Peacemaking*, Weidenfeld & Nicholson, London, 1968.
146   Nelson, K. L., *Victors Divided: America and the Allies in Germany, 1918–1923*, University of California Press, Berkeley, CA, 1975.
147   Schuker, S. A., *American 'Reparations' to Germany, 1919–1933*, Princeton University Press, Princeton, NJ, 1988.
148   Sharp, A., *The Versailles Settlement: Peacemaking in Paris, 1919*, St Martin's Press, 1991.
149   Trachtenberg, M., 'Reparation at the Paris peace conference', *Journal of Modern History*, 51, 1979, pp. 24–54.
150   Walworth, A. S., *America's Moment, 1918: American Diplomacy at the End of World War I*, W. W. Norton, 1977.

151 Walworth, A. S., *Wilson and His Peacemakers: American Diplomacy at the Paris Peace Conference, 1919*, W. W. Norton, 1986.

152 Widenor, W. C., *Henry Cabot Lodge and the Search for an American Foreign Policy*, University of California Press, Berkeley, CA, 1980.

153 Widenor, W. C., 'The United States and the Versailles Peace Settlement', in J. M. Carroll and G. C. Herring (eds), *Modern American Diplomacy*, Scholarly Resources, Wilmington, DE, 1996.

Social Reform

154 Bristow, N., *Making Men Moral: Social Engineering During the Great War*, New York University Press, 1996.

155 Chambers, III, J. W., *The Tyranny of Change: Americans in the Progressive Era, 1890–1920*, St Martin's Press, 1992.

156 Clark, N. H., *Deliver Us From Evil: An Interpretation of American Prohibition*, W. W. Norton, 1976.

157 Clark, N. H., *The Dry Years: Prohibition and Social Change in Washington*, University of Washington Press, Seattle, WA, 1988.

158 Davis, A. F., 'Welfare, reform, and World War I', *American Quarterly*, 19, 1967, pp. 516–33.

159 Dawley, A., *Struggles for Justice: Social Responsibility and the Liberal State*, Harvard University Press, Cambridge, MA, 1991.

160 Durham, W. B., '"Big brother" and the "seven sisters": camp life reforms in World War I', *Military Affairs*, April, 1978, pp. 516–33.

161 Goldman, E., *Rendezvous with Destiny: A History of Modern American Reform*, Knopf, 1956.

162 Graham, Jr., O. L., *The Great Campaigns: Reform and War in America, 1900–1928*, Prentice-Hall, Englewood Cliffs, NJ, 1971.

163 Higham, J., *Strangers in the Land*, Rutgers University Press, New Brunswick, NJ, 1988.

164 Kerr, K. A., *Organized for Prohibition: A New History of the Anti-Saloon League*, Yale University Press, New Haven, CT, 1985.

165 Link, A. S., *Woodrow Wilson and the Progressive Era, 1910–1917*, Harper, 1954.

166 Link, A. S. and R. L. McCormick, *Progressivism*, Harlan Davidson, Inc., Arlington Heights, IL, 1983.

167 Timberlake, J. H., *Prohibition and the Progressive Movement, 1900–1920*, Harvard University Press, Cambridge, MA, 1963.

168 Wynn, N. A., *From Progressivism to Prosperity: World War I and American Society*, Holmes & Meir, 1986.

Women

169 Chafe, W., *The American Woman: Her Changing Social, Economic, and Political Roles, 1920–1970*, Oxford University Press, 1972.

170 Davis, A. F., *American Heroine: The Life and Legend of Jane Addams*, Oxford University Press, 1973.

171   Dulles, F. R., *The American Red Cross. A History*, Greenwood Press, Westport, CT, 1971.
172   Evans, S. M., *Born for Liberty: A History of Women in America*, The Free Press, 1989.
173   Flexner, E., *Century of Struggle: The Woman's Rights Movement in the United States*, Atheneum, 1972.
174   Kraditor, A., *The Ideas of the Woman Suffrage Movement, 1890–1920*, Columbia University Press, 1965.
175   Schneider, D. and Schneider, C., *Into the Breach: American Women Overseas in World War I*, Viking Press, 1991.
176   Steinson, B.J., *American Women's Activism in World War I*, Garland Press, 1982.
177   Zeiger, S., 'She didn't raise her boy to be a slacker: motherhood, conscription, and the culture of the First World War', *Feminist Studies*, 22, 1996, pp. 6–39.

World Figures

178   Baker, R. S., *Woodrow Wilson; Life and Letters*, 8 vols, Greenwood Press, 1927–39.
179   Beaver, D. R., *Newton D. Baker and the American War Effort, 1917–1919*, University of Nebraska Press, Lincoln, NE, 1966.
180   Burner, D., *Herbert Hoover: A Public Life*, Knopf, 1984.
181   Clements, K. A., *Woodrow Wilson: World Statesman*, Twayne, Boston, MA, 1987.
182   Clements, K. A., *The Presidency of Woodrow Wilson*, University Press of Kansas, Lawrence, KS, 1992.
183   Cooper, J. M., *The Warrior and the Priest: Woodrow Wilson and Theodore Roosevelt*, Belknap Press of Harvard University Press, Cambridge MA, 1983.
184   Ferrell, R. H., *Woodrow Wilson and World War I, 1917–1921*, Harper & Row, 1985.
185   Harbaugh, H., *Power and Responsibility: The Life and Times of Theodore Roosevelt*, Farror, Straus, and Co., 1961.
186   Lockmiller, D. A., *Enoch H. Crowder: Soldier, Lawyer, Statesman*, Columbia University Press, 1955.
187   Nash, G., *The Life of Herbert Hoover*, 2 vols, W. W. Norton, 1983 & 1988.
188   Schulte-Nordholt, J. W., *Woodrow Wilson: A Life for Peace*, Meulenhoff, Amsterdam, 1991.
189   Smith, R. N., *An Uncommon Man: The Triumph of Herbert Hoover*, Simon and Schuster, 1984.
190   Smythe, D., *Pershing: General of the Armies*, Indiana University Press, Bloomington, IN, 1986.
191   Vandiver, F. E., *Black Jack: The Life and Times of John J. Pershing*, Texas A & M University Press, College Station, TX, 1977.
192   Weinstein, E. A., *Woodrow Wilson, a Medical and Psychological Biography*, Princeton University Press, Princeton, NJ, 1981.

World War I and Civil Liberties

193 Campbell, C. N., *Reel America and World War I: A Comprehensive Filmography*, McFarland Press, Jefferson, NC, 1985.

194 Coben, S., 'Postwar upheaval: the Red Scare', in A. Link (ed.), *The Impact of World War I*, Harper & Row, 1969.

195 Cornebeise, A., *War as Advertised: The Four Minute Men and America's Crusade, 1917–1918*, American Philosophical Society, Philadelphia, PA, 1984.

196 Creel, G., *How We Advertised America*, Arno Press, 1972.

197 Luebke, F. C., *The Bonds of Loyalty; German Americans and World War I*, Northern Illinois University Press, Dekalb, IL, 1974.

198 Mock, J. R. and Larsen, C., *Words that Won the War: The Story of the Committee on Public Information, 1917–1919*, Princeton University Press, Princeton, NJ, 1939.

199 Murphy, P. L., *World War I and the Origin of Civil Liberties in the United States*, W. W. Norton, 1979.

200 Murray, R., *Red Scare: A Study in National Hysteria, 1919–1920*, Greenwood Press, Westport, CT, 1980.

201 Peterson, H. C. and Fite, G. C., *Opponents of War, 1917–1918*, Greenwood Press, Westport, CT, 1986.

202 Preston, Jr., W., *Aliens and Dissenters: Federal Suppression of Radicals, 1903–1933*, University of Illinois Press, Urbana, IL, 1994.

203 Scheiber, H. N., *The Wilson Administration and Civil Liberties, 1917–1921*, Cornell University Press, Ithaca, 1960.

204 Vaughn, S. L., *Holding Fast the Inner Line: Democracy, Nationalism and the Committee on Public Information*, University of North Carolina Press, Chapel Hill, NC, 1980.

INDEX

STUART BRITAIN

Social Change and Continuity: England 1550–1750 (Second edition)
Barry Coward   0 582 29442 8

James I (Second edition)
S J Houston   0 582 20911 0

The English Civil War 1640–1649
Martyn Bennett   0 582 35392 0

Charles I, 1625–1640
Brian Quintrell   0 582 00354 7

The English Republic 1649–1660 (Second edition)
Toby Barnard   0 582 08003 7

Radical Puritans in England 1550–1660
R J Acheson   0 582 35515 X

The Restoration and the England of Charles II (Second edition)
John Miller   0 582 29223 9

The Glorious Revolution (Second edition)
John Miller   0 582 29222 0

EARLY MODERN EUROPE

The Renaissance (Second edition)
Alison Brown   0 582 30781 3

The Emperor Charles V
Martyn Rady   0 582 35475 7

French Renaissance Monarchy: Francis I and Henry II (Second edition)
Robert Knecht   0 582 28707 3

The Protestant Reformation in Europe
Andrew Johnston   0 582 07020 1

The French Wars of Religion 1559–1598 (Second edition)
Robert Knecht   0 582 28533 X

Phillip II
Geoffrey Woodward   0 582 07232 8

The Thirty Years' War
Peter Limm   0 582 35373 4

Louis XIV
Peter Campbell   0 582 01770 X

Spain in the Seventeenth Century
Graham Darby   0 582 07234 4

Peter the Great
William Marshall   0 582 00355 5

EUROPE 1789–1918

Britain and the French Revolution
Clive Emsley   0 582 36961 4

Revolution and Terror in France 1789–1795 (Second edition)
D G Wright   0 582 00379 2

Napoleon and Europe
D G Wright   0 582 35457 9

Nineteenth-Century Russia: Opposition to Autocracy
Derek Offord   0 582 35767 5

The Constitutional Monarchy in France 1814–48
Pamela Pilbeam   0 582 31210 8

The 1848 Revolutions (Second edition)
Peter Jones   0 582 06106 7

The Italian Risorgimento
M Clark   0 582 00353 9

Bismark & Germany 1862–1890 (Second edition)
D G Williamson   0 582 29321 9

Imperial Germany 1890–1918
Ian Porter, Ian Armour and Roger Lockyer   0 582 03496 5

The Dissolution of the Austro-Hungarian Empire 1867–1918 (Second edition)
John W Mason   0 582 29466 5

Second Empire and Commune: France 1848–1871 (Second edition)
William H C Smith   0 582 28705 7

France 1870–1914 (Second edition)
Robert Gildea   0 582 29221 2

The Scramble for Africa (Second edition)
M E Chamberlain   0 582 36881 2

Late Imperial Russia 1890–1917
John F Hutchinson   0 582 32721 0

The First World War
Stuart Robson   0 582 31556 5

EUROPE SINCE 1918

The Russian Revolution (Second edition)
Anthony Wood   0 582 35559 1

Lenin's Revolution: Russia, 1917–1921
David Marples   0 582 31917 X

Stalin and Stalinism (Second edition)
Martin McCauley   0 582 27658 6

The Weimar Republic (Second edition)
John Hiden   0 582 28706 5

The Inter-War Crisis 1919–1939
Richard Overy   0 582 35379 3

Fascism and the Right in Europe, 1919–1945
Martin Blinkhorn   0 582 07021 X

Spain's Civil War (Second edition)
Harry Browne   0 582 28988 2

The Third Reich (Second edition)
D G Williamson   0 582 20914 5

The Origins of the Second World War (Second edition)
R J Overy   0 582 29085 6

The Second World War in Europe
Paul MacKenzie   0 582 32692 3

Anti-Semitism before the Holocaust
Albert S Lindemann   0 582 36964 9

The Holocaust: The Third Reich and the Jews
David Engel   0 582 32720 2

Britain and Europe since 1945
Alex May   0 582 30778 3

Eastern Europe 1945–1969: From Stalinism to Stagnation
Ben Fowkes   0 582 32693 1

The Khrushchev Era, 1953–1964
Martin McCauley   0 582 27776 0

NINETEENTH-CENTURY BRITAIN

Britain before the Reform Acts: Politics and Society 1815–1832
Eric J Evans   0 582 00265 6

Parliamentary Reform in Britain c. 1770–1918
Eric J Evans   0 582 29467 3

Democracy and Reform 1815–1885
D G Wright   0 582 31400 3

Poverty and Poor Law Reform in Nineteenth-Century Britain, 1834–1914:
From Chadwick to Booth
David Englander   0 582 31554 9

The Birth of Industrial Britain: Economic Change, 1750–1850
Kenneth Morgan   0 582 29833 4

Chartism (Third edition)
Edward Royle   0 582 29080 5

Peel and the Conservative Party 1830–1850
Paul Adelman   0 582 35557 5

Gladstone, Disraeli and later Victorian Politics (Third edition)
Paul Adelman   0 582 29322 7

Britain and Ireland: From Home Rule to Independence
Jeremy Smith   0 582 30193 9

TWENTIETH-CENTURY BRITAIN

The Rise of the Labour Party 1880–1945 (Third edition)
Paul Adelman   0 582 29210 7

The Conservative Party and British Politics 1902–1951
Stuart Ball   0 582 08002 9

The Decline of the Liberal Party 1910–1931 (Second edition)
Paul Adelman   0 582 27733 7

The British Women's Suffrage Campaign 1866–1928
Harold L Smith   0 582 29811 3

War & Society in Britain 1899–1948
Rex Pope   0 582 03531 7

The British Economy since 1914: A Study in Decline?
Rex Pope   0 582 30194 7

Unemployment in Britain between the Wars
Stephen Constantine   0 582 35232 0

The Attlee Governments 1945–1951
Kevin Jefferys   0 582 06105 9

The Conservative Governments 1951–1964
Andrew Boxer   0 582 20913 7

Britain under Thatcher
Anthony Seldon and Daniel Collings   0 582 31714 2

INTERNATIONAL HISTORY

The Eastern Question 1774–1923 (Second edition)
A L Macfie   0 582 29195 X

The Origins of the First World War (Second edition)
Gordon Martel   0 582 28697 2

The United States and the First World War
Jennifer D Keene   0 582 35620 2

Anti-Semitism before the Holocaust
Albert S Lindemann   0 582 36964 9

The Origins of the Cold War, 1941–1949 (Second edition)
Martin McCauley   0 582 27659 4

Russia, America and the Cold War, 1949–1991
Martin McCauley   0 582 27936 4

The Arab–Israeli Conflict
Kirsten E Schulze   0 582 31646 4

The United Nations since 1945: Peacekeeping and the Cold War
Norrie MacQueen   0 582 35673 3

Decolonisation: The British Experience since 1945
Nicholas J White   0 582 29087 2

The Vietnam War
Mitchell Hall   0 582 32859 4

WORLD HISTORY

China in Transformation 1900–1949
Colin Mackerras   0 582 31209 4

US HISTORY

America in the Progressive Era, 1890–1914
Lewis L Gould   0 582 35671 7

The United States and the First World War
Jennifer D Keene   0 582 35620 2

The Truman Years, 1945–1953
Mark S Byrnes   0 582 32904 3

The Vietnam War
Mitchell Hall   0 582 32859 4